Tools for Critique

to Explore

Teaching to Change the World

Second Edition

Jeannie Oakes
University of California, Los Angeles

Martin Lipton
University of California, Los Angeles

Prepared by
Jeannie Oakes
University of California, Los Angeles

Martin Lipton
University of California, Los Angeles

Jamy Stillman
University of California, Los Angeles

Boston   Burr Ridge, IL   Dubuque, IA   Madison, WI   New York   San Francisco   St. Louis
Bangkok   Bogotá   Caracas   Kuala Lumpur   Lisbon   London   Madrid   Mexico City
Milan   Montreal   New Delhi   Santiago   Seoul   Singapore   Sydney   Taipei   Toronto

The McGraw·Hill Companies

Tools for Critique to Explore
TEACHING TO CHANGE THE WORLD
Jeannie Oakes, Martin Lipton

Published by McGraw-Hill, an imprint of The McGraw-Hill Companies, Inc., 1221 Avenue of the Americas, New York, NY 10020. Copyright © 2003 by The McGraw-Hill Companies, Inc.

2 3 4 5 6 7 8 9 0 QSR/QSR 0 9 8 7 6 5 4 3 2

ISBN 0-07-240739-5

www.mhhe.com

CONTENTS

OVERVIEW OF THE TEXT

Teaching to Change the World provides a comprehensive exploration of teaching for twenty-first century American schools. It is both practical and foundational. Each chapter describes a particular domain of school knowledge and practice—learning, curriculum, instruction, classroom management, school culture, and so on. Each emphasizes how the historical, philosophical, and sociological foundations of education are alive and well in the everyday practices of today's schools. Rather than treating these foundations as interesting background or "enrichment," the authors use them as powerful, sense-making tools that illuminate contemporary schooling practices and concerns.

SOCIOCULTURAL THEORY IN A MULTICULTURAL SOCIETY

Teaching to Change the World responds to the current national crisis in teaching and teacher education by taking up the challenge set forth by the National Commission on Teaching and America's Future. Study director Linda Darling-Hammond calls for teacher educators to address "the nation's need for powerful teaching that is available to all students, not just the affluent and lucky; and the need for the strategies that can help sustain such teaching in schools organized for serious learning for all students, not just an elite minority."

Unlike other introductory and foundational texts, *Teaching to Change the World* doesn't simply offer a smorgasbord of theory for readers to browse, choosing whatever suits their appetites. Rather, the book represents a new genre in teacher education texts. In addition to providing a solid research base and practical treatment of the essential topics of traditional texts, it offers a groundbreaking approach that locates these topics within cognitive, sociocultural, and constructivist perspectives on learning, and within democratic values. Indeed, two themes weave the chapters into a coherent story: the first theme is that learning is a social and cultural activity; the second theme is that the United States is a multicultural society.

CRITICAL QUESTIONS

The authors do not approach schooling as neutral, or teaching as a neutral profession. *Teaching to Change the World* has a point of view. Its roots lie in John Dewey's turn of the twentieth-century learning theories and political sentiments, and its current frames of reference are the sociocultural and democratic theorists who are Dewey's intellectual descendants at the beginning of the twenty-first century. The book takes the position that a hopeful, democratic future depends on whether all students learn and experience academic rigor and social justice in school. If good teaching and rigorous academic achievement do not reach every student in every class, we lock out the possibility of both social justice and excellence, even for a few. It is not sufficient for good teachers to possess appropriate professional skills and impart the culture's knowledge and values to students. Throughout, the text emphasizes research and historical analyses that show how excellent teaching requires social justice.

Teaching to Change the World aims to help teachers understand what is good in education, and to dissuade them from simply getting good at what is popular. It provides a solid professional groundwork of social theory and educational research. Its social-justice perspective brings three critical elements to teachers' professional knowledge:

- The text considers the values and politics that pervade education, as well as the more technical issues of teaching and organizing schools.

- It asks critical questions about how conventional thinking and practice came to be, and who in society benefits from them.
- It pays particular attention to inequalities associated with race, social class, language, gender, and other social categories, and looks for alternatives to the inequalities.

STRUGGLE SUSTAINED BY HOPE

Teaching to Change the World depicts teachers' efforts to achieve social justice in their teaching as a struggle sustained by hope. Lacking hope, many thousands of promising teachers quit the profession within their first few years, unable to see how they can make a difference in students' lives. This book helps to build a foundation for hope by helping teachers understand and critique "common sense" views of schools and conventional practices. The book makes the foundations relevant and encourages students to their reveal their hope, idealism, questions, and "silent reservations" about equity-minded teaching.

THE STUDENT VOICE

Teaching to Change the World pulls no punches and invites lively discussion and debate. Students find it provocative and sometimes irritating, but engaging and interesting to read and learn from. Throughout the chapters are boxed observations of a diverse group of first-year teachers—in their own words, taken from the comprehensive portfolios they presented for their Masters Degree in Education and teaching certification program at UCLA. As one would expect, these teachers are struggling with lesson plans, discipline, paperwork, time management, school bureaucracy, and so on. But what is particularly engaging about these teachers is not that they struggle, but the quality of the problems with which they struggle. These teachers belie one criticism of a social-justice emphasis to a teacher's career—that these are soft "do-gooders" whose social agenda wipes out their obligation to teach. Their reflections reveal the profound relevance of theory to their practice and to their mostly successful, often joyful, efforts to sustain their combined commitment to rigorous instruction and social justice.

ABOUT THIS GUIDE

Teaching to Change the World asks prospective teachers to think very differently about teaching K-12 students. This guide presumes that their professors are already thinking differently about teaching and guiding college students. And just as the text situates K-12 teachers' pedagogy in a context of inquiry, struggle, and hope (rather than surefire "best practice"), this guide addresses elements of their professors' thinking and practice that look first to engage students in inquiry, struggle, and hope rather than transmit educational facts. Consequently, you will find, for example, no "true/false" tests on authentic instruction; no quizzes asking students to match educational vocabulary with definitions in order to assess the students' knowledge of rich and deep curriculum; and no lecture notes for cooperative learning.

The remainder of the guide is divided into two sections. The first section suggests a teaching approach—a set of pedagogical principles—and types of learning activities that match those recommended in the text itself. The second section provides chapter-specific overviews, outlines, lists of "generative" questions and activities, a sampling of Internet resources that can be used as a basis for learning and assessment tasks, and video-related activities.

Throughout, we make little distinction between activities and questions on the one hand, and student assessment and accountability on the other hand. We trust that faculty using this text will struggle to find adequate ways to measure, rank, and grade their students (or to avoid these practices altogether) in ways that are consistent with the exigencies of their school and department administrations; their job security; and their time, resources, and class size.

TEACHING APPROACH

PRINCIPLES FOR CONSTRUCTING (AND DECONSTRUCTING) LEARNING ACTIVITIES AND QUESTIONS

This guide attempts to follow the principles of instruction and assessment discussed in Chapters 6 and 7 of *Teaching to Change the World*. Accordingly, the suggestions offered here—to be modified to suit each professor's unique context—can support a pedagogy in the college classroom that is constructivist, sociocultural, and oriented toward considerations of social justice in schooling. Ideally, these activities and questions can help faculty create settings for prospective teachers that match those where people learn naturally, at the same time as they promote the intellectual quality and the authenticity of students' academic work. In suggesting activities and questions, we have kept in mind the following principles, and we offer them here to assist in further modifications and in the construction of your own activities and questions.

- **"Meta-instruction"—make your own constructions and struggles transparent**. Initially, it is unlikely that students enrolled in an introductory or survey course in education will feel and act like anything other than traditional students—relying on their traditional conceptions of proper student roles, distribution of power, "old reliable" coping mechanisms and habits, and so on. If they continue to function from within that traditional student role, *Teaching to Change the World* could distance students from sociocultural perspectives rather than engage them deeply in those perspectives. Consider sharing each of the following principles with students (as stated below or modified). For example, ask students to explore the degree to which an assignment or question you have asked engages them in authentic work. For self or peer assessments, ask them for evidence of disciplined inquiry. Ask students to join you in monitoring class activities for potential opportunities (or the lack of them) to build on differences, and so on. Continue to emphasize the *generative* (meaning something very close to *constructive)* nature of assessment/instructional questions. That is, without evading a query that can be resolved with empirical evidence, students should develop skills to recognize the positivism and reductionism that inevitably creeps into questions designed to direct another's thinking. Finally, you can assure students that the *struggle* for a sociocultural pedagogy does not guarantee teaching perfection—theirs or yours.

- **Engage students in authentic work.** Following Fred Newman's research (described in Chapter 6), we suggest activities that help students construct knowledge, use disciplined inquiry, and see that what they are learning has value and meaning beyond their coursework. Constructing knowledge brings students' learning in the college classroom closer to the kind of learning—for example, solving complex and ill-structured problems—that successful teachers engage in as they think about and make decisions regarding their work with students. Disciplined inquiry respects students' prior knowledge and experience and presses students to build on that prior knowledge base. Those who carry out such inquiry strive to understand deeply prior knowledge and experience, subject understandings to the critiques of colleagues, reflect upon them in light of educational research and theory, communicate them articulately, and express them in action.

- **Build on difference.** Activities recommended in this guide follow from the premise that college classrooms—like K-12 classrooms—can be communities of very diverse learners where everybody is smart, and where differences are the source of rich learning interactions. Faculty can work toward making each student's particular competence visible and available to others as a learning resource. Social interactions allow students to scaffold one another's learning and to combine their different knowledge and experiences into the learning community's knowledge and experience. Such activities are meant to support a positive cycle of confidence, effort, persistence, and learning for all class members. The goal is for students to assume that everyone is competent; that it is everyone's job to help everyone contribute; and that individual competence is contingent upon participating in the classroom learning community.

- **Create active and multidimensional learning opportunities.** The suggested activities and questions are meant to engage students in learning by doing, not simply by reading and writing about the ideas in the text. Most of the generative questions—interesting enough for a traditional class discussion—can be modified to become complex, long-range, collaborative projects that allow for more than one answer or more than one approach to problem finding and solving.

- **Provide scaffolding.** The role of the teacher, and to some degree, of a classmate, is to support or "scaffold" students as they move through their "zone of proximal development," defined as the knowledge and skills that the student cannot learn on his own, but can learn with the assistance (scaffolding) of someone who is more capable. As with an apprentice's relationship to an accomplished member of the community, all contributions—no matter how small—that a novice might make are valued. Interactions that lead students to develop new insights, deeper understandings, and greater thinking skills are those in which a teacher or a classmate presses the students through questioning and sharing of ideas to go beyond their current thinking.

- **Prompt substantive conversations.** In the framework of authentic instruction, "students engage in extended conversational exchanges with the teacher and/or their peers about subject matter in a way that builds an improved or shared understanding of ideas or topics."[1] Such conversations go far beyond reporting facts, procedures, or definitions to focus on making distinctions, applying ideas, forming generalizations, and raising questions. Substantive conversations are not scripted or controlled. Rather, they flow from a sharing of ideas among the participants. The conversation builds on or extends important themes and principles the teacher has decided are essential for all to know, rather than settling for "reinforcing" (i.e., learning intact) the facts and concepts required for minimum recall or competence.

---

[1] Newman, authentic instruction, see chapter 6 note

- **Dig deeper.** Each chapter in the text ends with a section called "Digging Deeper." Here we identify scholars who are studying or working on practical applications of the issues we raise, and we list a few of their books and articles that you and/or your students might find interesting and useful. In some chapters, we also list professional organizations and activist groups working to make education policy or school practices more consistent with and supportive of socially just teaching. Wherever possible, we provide Internet sites that provide good starting points for pursuing their work and finding other resources. Students would certainly benefit from exposure to these generally more academic pieces that provide a finer grained treatment of some aspect of the chapter.

BANK OF GENERATIVE QUESTIONS AND ACTIVITIES

For each chapter, we propose a list of questions and prompts that faculty can modify, adapt, and, certainly, improve for their particular students and purposes. The questions are written chronologically and are organized according to the chapter main headings. These questions can generate class discussions that stretch students to make sense of the material in ways that go beyond simply repeating or summarizing it. The questions can also serve as prompts for other in- and out-of-class activities and assignments that support the principles listed above.

When using the questions, keep in mind that a chapter may revisit concepts introduced earlier (or in Bruner's terms, concepts "spiral" throughout the text). Consequently, many of the questions introduced in earlier chapters can be useful again later in the term. Similarly, questions in later chapters may prompt returning to earlier chapters. It is, of course, everyone's wish that students' perspectives will change and their understanding and arguments will become more refined as the course proceeds.

Generally, the questions ask students to respond to a concept introduced in the text by reflecting on the student's own experience or observation. We do not intend to make an unwarranted distinction between experience and observation—simply to extend the range of legitimate student responses. In other words, anything that students experience themselves or see happening to others—past or present—can be fodder for these reflections. To further invite "universal" participation (in case some students would excuse themselves by claiming that they have neither experienced nor observed relevant events), most of the questions can be modified by adding the element, "What would you think if you were to experience or see. . . ." Indeed, some of the questions call for speculation and, in groups, brainstorming. Further, while we call for steady attention to "disciplined inquiry," we recognize that these generative questions are large and spill over into many disciplines. Inquiry into any one of them is more likely to be ended with, "Sorry, but we must move on. . . ." than with "Now that everyone is satisfied with the answer. . . ." We do not worry that students will miss out on educational facts or truth. Again, Bruner's spiral is instructive. Although we are interested in building an early foundation for future study that is based on sociocultural and social justice perspectives, we are convinced that this will happen only if students, and later, teachers, return again and again to re-examine salient educational issues.

Most faculty will prefer to preselect, modify, and pace how students use these and other generative questions. However, there is also value in encouraging students to consider (and critique) many more of the questions than they will personally be responsible for answering, to allow choices among questions, to encourage different students to answer and perhaps lead discussions or different questions, and so on. The list below suggests some specific strategies for engaging students authentically both in and out of class. **Generative questions can**:

- Prompt 5- to 10-minute in-class **"quick writes"** that allow students to recall and focus on the material at the beginning of class, provide faculty with a way of holding students accountable for assigned reading, provide a "thinking break" during class, or serve as a reflective closing activity.

- Frame small, **cooperative group learning** activities. A good rule of thumb is that each class meeting can provide each student with the opportunity to speak, question, and respond. Nearly all students—especially those who are contemplating a teaching career—will profit from engaging others in problem finding and problem solving around complex and challenging issues. While students may learn about cooperative groups as a teaching *method*, too many students enter the profession with astonishing little actual group experience—which is to say, too few have skills in functioning as productive group members. Effective teachers need enough group experiences to acquire a deep understanding of cooperative group structures, methods of achieving diversity within groups, interdependent goal and reward structures, and more. And although we are oversimplifying here, students must experience how activity— *participation*—as a valued member of the group is inseparable from *knowledge* learned in the group. A final suggestion is to encourage college students to continue their collaborative work outside class meetings.

- Be used as **reflective writing** topics. Students' own K-12 schooling experiences (and those of their parents and friends) will act inevitably as powerful filters as they attempt to make sense of the ideas presented in the text. Reflective writing outside of class can help students bridge their personal, informal, experiential knowledge of schooling with ideas in the text that may challenge that knowledge. Students can keep journals wherein they make these connections, confrontations, and contradictions explicit. Many of the generative questions for each chapter can serve as prompts for reflective journal entries, or a standard prompt might be used that has students revisit the same question each week. Reflective writing can be maintained as private writing or shared with the instructor and/or peers.

- Initiate **electronic conversations** or **interactive journals**. Students often report that they learn more from the diverse experiences and reactions of their peers to course material than they do from formal class activities. To capitalize on this potent source of scaffolding, students can be paired each week as "respondents" to each other's reflective writing. Some instructors establish online "news groups" for the class, so that everyone has access to everyone else's writings and responses. If the class is small enough, faculty may also wish to respond weekly to each student's reflective writing. Alternatively, faculty may respond to a few students each week, reacting to all of them once or twice over the course of the term. Writing can be exchanged either on paper or by electronic mail. Not incidentally, online writing provides an efficient way to document and assess students' growth in thinking about the text material over the course of the term.

- Focus students' **case studies of K-12 students**. Teacher education students can use a term-long case-study project to better understand how students' experiences at school connect with the material in *Teaching to Change the World*. Each chapter raises particular issues that, by the term's end, will allow students to consider the complexity of teaching and learning in today's schools and explore how they play out in the lives of students. In diverse communities, it is particularly useful if students select a K-12 student whose race, language, or culture is different from their own. That way, prospective teachers will have a guided experience in respectfully learning about students from within the students' own social and environmental contexts. Students can "shadow" a student in order to get a sense of his or her experiences during and after school. They can engage in conversations with the student and his or her family, including making a home visit. If the case study is designed as a major course project, students can write a final analytic paper capturing the essence of what they've learned. The paper can include a rich, thick description of the K-12 student, supported with "evidence" from the student's own words or with field notes. To do this, students will need to read carefully "between the lines" of the facts they've collected about the student for *themes* (beneath-the-surface meanings derived from the particulars of the case). They can review the ideas in the text for insights into what their "data" might mean from a theoretical perspective. They can search their data for evidence that both confirms and challenges the themes and theories—going back and forth between reading the data and reviewing the course readings. Case-study assignments also provide student first-hand experience with a method that researchers and professionals use when they want to understand a complex phenomenon— such as students' schooling experiences—and how that phenomenon is a part of a larger context, such as home, culture, and social structures.

- Guide students' **interviews of educators or school community members**. Many college students have considerable difficulty understanding the intersection of educational theory and school practices. So do most teachers. However, students begin to see how the larger issues of schooling and society play out in everyday school events and in teachers' lives when the students engage educators, parents, school board members, or other adults in a school community in considering the issues posed in the generative questions.

- Serve as the basis of **assessment tasks**. Assessment, like instruction, must be authentic, reflective, and interactive, and it must provide multiple routes to success. Just like instruction, assessment should prompt students to put some of their thinking into language, sort their knowledge into sequences, and form whole impressions and conclusions. As students construct logical answers that include descriptions, facts, experiences, and problems, they use their knowledge. This gives them access to richer and more complex knowledge than they could gain by repeating facts they heard or recognizing and choosing the correct answer on a test. When teacher and student go back and forth during assessments, there are more ways for the teacher to help the student express what he knows. Interactions can be open-ended. When teachers ask students probing questions such as, "What do you think of that?" "What will you do next?" "Why did you do it that way?" and "How did you figure that out?" they get as close as they can to the heart of the student's learning. The student's responses will reveal his sense-making—not just his conclusions. Portfolios are often profitably integrated in an overall plan for authentic assessment. They work especially well when they go beyond simple collections of all the student's work and require students to make their own evaluative judgments about their own growth and best work. If students receive feedback in the form of new questions and encouragement, it prompts them to push beyond their first hunches.

WEB SITES

For each chapter we provide a list of sample Web sites that are useful in their own right and indicate a range of background reading for students. Because sites are subject to change, we recommend accessing these links through **McGraw-Hill's home page,[[AU: URL?]]** where we will be posting updates.

More subtle, but also more challenging, is determining the source, accuracy, and value of the material included on sites. Part of the amazement of the Internet is its fundamental democracy. Anyone can create a Web page with anything on it. That means that scholars and instructors using the Internet can't rely on the conventions of print publishing—for example, peer-review processes, reputation of journal or publisher, published reviews, and so on—as indicators of the quality of the material. We urge instructors to pass along these same quality-control caveats to their students.

The nonlinear quality of the Web, too, is a wonderful and complicating feature. So note that, while we've listed Web sites under the chapters where they seem to belong at first glance, many include links to other sites that are relevant to other chapters in the book. Many of the sites also include additional links that are worth pursuing. We've only scratched the surface of what was available in the summer of 2002, and we've probably missed many of the best sites.

One useful resource for helping to understand and navigate the Internet in conjunction with education research and teaching is David M. Fetterman's article "Webs of Meaning: Computer and Internet Resources for Educational Research and Instruction," which appeared in *Educational Researcher* in April 1998 (vol. 27, no. 3, pp. 22–30.) Author Fetterman also lists a number of Web sites related to current education policy issues at **http://www.stanford.edu/~davidf/policylist.html**. Fetterman recommends Arizona State University Professor Gene Glass's education resource page at **http://www.ed.asu.edu/coe/links/old_links**. Other basic resources are the U.S. Department of Education site at **http://www.ed.gov/**; *Education Week* on the Web at **http://www.edweek.org**, the American Association of Educational Research site at **http://aera.net**, and the ERIC system "Ask ERIC" search engine for education resources at **http://ericir.syr.edu**. **http://www.newhorizons.org** is an especially noteworthy site with extensive articles and bibliographies. Dedicated to "Equal Opportunity for the Development of Human Capacities," the site offers foundational support for many education topics.

THE *ONLY A TEACHER* VIDEO SERIES

The documentary series ***Only A Teacher*** traces the history of American public schools and teachers from the beginning of the nineteenth century to the present. The three one-hour episodes, *A Teacher Affects Eternity, Those Who Can . . . Teach,* and *Teaching to End Inequity,* explore many of the same issues addressed in *Teaching to Change the World* and can be used as effective teaching tools in conjunction with this text. Through the portrayal of teachers' voices, both past and present, the series demonstrates how current debates about policy, curriculum, the role of the teacher, and educational equity find their roots in the emergence of the common school and longstanding beliefs about the purpose of education. Go to http://www.pbs.org/onlyateacher/about.html for more information about the series.

For most of the chapters, we provide questions and activities that tie the themes from *Teaching to Change the World* to the *Only a Teacher* video series. You may wish to show the videos in their entirety, but the questions can also be used delve more deeply into particular video segments and corresponding sections of the text.

VIDEOS

Some of the chapters also include generative questions and activities that refer to videos other than those in the *Only a Teacher* series. A list of these references is provided at the end of each of these chapters.

CHAPTER-BY-CHAPTER GUIDES

In the sections that follow, we've reproduced the chapter overviews that students will find in the Introduction to the text and a list of the chapter headings, including the page numbers in the text on which the topics appear. Together these summarize each chapter's primary focus and structure. The bank of generative questions for each chapter are listed in the order in which the topics and issues they address appear in the chapter.

CHAPTER 1
SCHOOLING: WRESTLING WITH TRADITION

OVERVIEW

Chapter 1, "Schooling: Wrestling with Tradition," explains the conflict within Americans as they both pursue and avoid the ideal of the "common school." We probe four deeply held modern beliefs—the myths of merit, efficiency, competition, and progress—that insulate schools from crucial research and practices. The first, *merit*, is the belief that people deserve what they have, and if they have little, that is all they deserve. The second, *factory efficiency*, is the belief that a rational, scientifically run organization geared to produce the greatest return, outcome, or "bottom line" benefits everyone working within that system. The third, *marketplace competition*, claims that social benefits are fairly and justly distributed through unfettered competition. Fourth and finally, *progress* suggests that current practices result from a progression of improvements and that only further improvement and "fine-tuning" of these practices is necessary.

The chapter concludes with arguments that each of these cultural beliefs has been tested in schools and is collapsing under global, postmodern demands for a skilled, flexible, and diverse citizenry. Meeting the demands of the twenty-first century in the democratic spirit of the common school requires the preeminence of a fifth American cultural belief that comes to Americans from our shared heritage of slavery: *struggle*. To *struggle* is to direct one's unflinching commitment, endurance, and hope in order to achieve social justice. In a world that does not promise moral victories, struggle promises a moral journey.

1

CHAPTER HEADINGS

GENERATIVE QUESTIONS AND ACTIVITIES

Schooling: *Wrestling with Tradition*

1. What do you think of Mary Ann Pacheco's wish to have her students learn that they have the power to change things, and of her decision to share with them her own reasons for becoming a teacher? Are these appropriate matters to discuss with students—first and second graders, in particular? Considering the chapter's title, what objections might tradition-minded people raise to Pacheco's treatment of this subject? Recall instances from your own schooling

in which a teacher revealed a deeply personal sentiment or motive. What was the effect on you and on the class?

The Teaching Challenge of the Twenty-First Century

2. When first-year teacher Michelle Calva asks, "What exactly is our obligation to prepare my students for the future?" she clearly has a particular multicultural future in mind. How would you answer her question? To what or to whom do you suppose she is referring when she speaks of the "dominant society"? Why and in what ways are you a member of the dominant society? In what ways are you not?

A Brief History of American Public Schools

3. Return to the "tough cultural questions" progressives are likely to ask: "Whose schools are these, and who benefits from them?" "Whose language may be spoken?" "Whose knowledge is important to include?" Why are these important questions? How would you answer them? Are you inclined to distinguish between "cultural" knowledge, such as that which might be presented in a social studies class, and "factual" knowledge, such as that contained in mathematics and science classes? Should a new teacher be certain of the answers to these questions before beginning teaching? Should experienced teachers be certain of the answers?

4. ***Only* a Teacher**. The first segment of the video *A Teacher Affects Eternity*, also entitled, "A Teacher Affects Eternity," touches on many of the themes covered by Oakes and Lipton in Chapter 1. Kathleen Weiler, one of the scholars appearing in the video, speaks about schools as mechanisms that support economic stability. She posits that the common school and common curriculum emerged to prevent the working classes from rebelling against their bosses, thus undermining the capitalist economy. Do you believe this to be true? Why or why not? What evidence do you see of this in schools today?

5. ***Only* a Teacher**. According to "Assimilating the Alien," a segment from the *A Teacher Affects Eternity* video, and authors Oakes and Lipton, schools at the end of the nineteenth century were institutions that preserved culture in addition to maintaining patterns of economic distribution. Do you believe that schools today generally still share this purpose of cultural and economic preservation? What evidence do you have (from current policy debates) to support your position? Can you find some exceptions to your general view?

6. ***Only* a Teacher**. *A Teacher Affects Eternity* also considers late nineteenth and early twentieth century schools and teachers as responsible for "Saving Souls." Do you suppose that this was strictly a spiritual concern, or did society's leaders hope that "saving souls" also would address the social and cultural fears that occupied these leaders? Do you think that schools can be effective in developing students' spiritual and moral sensibilities without simultaneously addressing

social, economic, and political concerns? In your opinion, to what degree, if any, can conditions such as poverty, racism, inequality, urban decay, and cultural unrest be addressed by instruction that targets students' moral codes and individual virtue?

7. ***Only a Teacher***. Oakes and Lipton also argue that conservatives' partial answer to poor school performance is to provide "character education" and instill "traditional values." Considering the "Assimilating the Alien" segment of the *A Teacher Affects Eternity* video, can this emphasis on character and tradition be considered a form of assimilation? Why and/or why not?

8. From newspapers, magazines, and other sources, begin collecting evidence of "complex political battles" that affect schooling in your (or any) community. At some point you may narrow your collection, becoming more selective as to topic, but for now, collect as much as you can to simply get a sense of the scope of the controversies. After you and your colleagues have amassed a large collection, sort them into preliminary categories of disputes (e.g., dominant versus subdominant cultures, politically liberal versus politically conservative perspectives, and other categories that will occur as you continue reading).

9. How did you learn about democratic behavior? Of course, this is an impossibly complex question, but try to identify several specific experiences in democratic practice (at home, at play, in the community, at school, at work, etc.) that probably contributed to developing your democratic sensibilities.

10. Consider two different emphases that schools might take to promote a democratic society: first, to teach students to change society so that it is more fair and democratic; and second, to teach students to fit into a society that, if not perfect, is pretty much worth keeping as it is. Few people would argue that either of these emphases should be excluded, and most would claim to have a vision that could accomplish both; however, most people would lean toward one of the two positions. Which position are you inclined to favor?

11. What do you suppose will happen to the "value" of your own college degree once college becomes the norm instead of a credential for the elite? In what ways is a "good education" a relative matter—that is, how does being well educated sometimes mean being better educated than someone else? What are some of the social and individual consequences of this relative definition of a good education?

12. Have you ever wondered why governments seem unable or unwilling to provide children of poorer parents with schools that are as well equipped and teachers who are as well qualified as those intended for children of wealthier parents? How can you explain this?

13. Consider first-year teacher Matthew Eide's questions again (p. 9). "How do issues of race, class, and gender influence what I do? How does my classroom resist and perpetuate the institutional racism, classism, linguicism, and sexism of education and society?" Recall teachers you have known who might have struggled with questions such as these. Have you had teachers who seemed

to value diversity more than most teachers? How would you describe your relationships with those teachers and, if you were a student in their classes, your experiences in those classes? In what ways were you more, or less, engaged in the subject matter than you were in other classes?

14. "Acceptable" or polite language changes with the times. When Thomas Jefferson wrote, "The best geniuses will be raked from the rubbish," the impact on a reader was probably not the same as it is today. Even so, this is pretty strong language. Do you think sentiments like this one exist today? How might today's schools serve as "rakes" with the goal of separating the best students from the "rubbish"? Note the attitudes behind specific schooling practices you have observed or experienced. Also note particular schooling efforts designed to counteract Jefferson's geniuses/rubbish dichotomy.

15. Oakes and Lipton briefly trace some of the historical links between racism and conceptions of intelligence (and provide further background in Chapter 2). How much of this history did you already know? Is such background information appropriate for students to learn in their K-12 schooling? In your own schooling, did you ever learn about these historical explanations of race and the qualities that were attributed to race?

16. Many people who are personally horrified by the existence of racial prejudice and believe themselves to be free of it are surprised to learn how extensive, logical, and scientific sounding are the arguments prejudiced people use to support their beliefs. Describe a person you know who cannot be swayed

from a belief in the fundamental inferiority of one or more groups of people. Provide this person's arguments in as much detail as possible. (Hint: One of the true challenges of a skilled interviewer/researcher is the ability to keep the interviewee talking—revealing information—when the interviewer has strong feelings about the content and may even be seething inside.)

17. Any exploration of racism in the United States is bound to be long, complex, deep, and uncomfortable—even painful. Why do you think that is? And because a single discussion neither eliminates experience nor changes society, such conversations require extraordinary patience, goodwill, and endurance. Try talking about these difficulties with someone of your own race. Then try talking about them with someone whose race differs from yours. Were the conversations different? In what way? How do you make sense of any differences?

18. Describe racism that you experienced or witnessed in school. Some people tend to see a certain "equality" in racism—finding all racism basically alike and equally deplorable. For example, they might consider racial conflicts between African Americans and Latino students (or teachers) and those between whites and other races to be essentially the same. They may go so far as to say that "since everyone has prejudices," we cannot suggest that any one group has a greater responsibility for changing its attitudes than any other group. . Other people, while not condoning any racist behaviors, believe that racist attitudes can never be separated from the relative power that

groups have in society in general. People with this view would say that racist actions taken by groups with the most power, such as whites, are more serious and damaging than racist actions taken by less powerful groups. Do your experiences lead you to one of these positions?

19. Consider the anti-immigrant measures highlighted by Oakes and Lipton (such as California's Propositions 187 and 227). As a teacher of students who might be affected by these laws, what do you see as your role? Would you comply? Resist? Perhaps a combination of both? To what degree would you involve your students in the struggle? Is involving the students appropriate/ professional?

20. The latter half of the twentieth century has seen increasing "privatization" of many previously public services. Corporations such as Federal Express do work previously done by the Post Office; private security services guard some neighborhoods previously watched over by the police; and private K-12 schooling is increasingly promoted as preferable to public education. What do you think of these trends? Do they threaten, enhance, or have no bearing on the common interests in a democracy?

21. Jonathon Kozol writes of "savage inequalities" between the education offered to poor minority students and that offered to middle-class white students. What makes these particular inequalities so starkly horrifying is that they often exist within the same community—perhaps just across a street. You may notice a contrast of opportunities within your community, or one with which you are

familiar. Describe this contrast. What "deficit" explanations might a person use to argue that these conditions are essentially the fault of students and their parents, rather than unfair institutions or prejudice?

22. Oakes and Lipton assert, "It is unthinkable that the nation would tolerate a lack of textbooks in an entire urban school district . . . if its children were white and not poor" (p. 14). Do you agree? Visit a "resource-rich" school in an affluent neighborhood. Describe the conditions there, paying particular attention to facilities, books, teacher qualifications, class size, how demanding the curriculum is, and so on. Focus on those elements that you think an "ordinary" or poor school might lack. Similarly, seek out a school that serves poor children, but has a reputation for being well equipped with resources and having well-qualified teachers. Compare this school with a school in an affluent neighborhood. Are there similarities? Are there subtle differences? Do an Internet search to see how much of this information is on-line for your state.

23. Oakes and Lipton describe several examples of lawsuits that attempted to make educational equity and "adequacy" legal requirements. Yet they also assert that taking legal action is only the first step. Decisions such as 1954's *Brown v. Board of Education* show the importance but also the limitations of court decisions. If this is true, what needs to happen in addition to legal action? On a policy level? On a community level? On a teacher level? Investigate one of the educational equity cases from the late twentieth or early twenty-first century. Consider what additional work will be

needed at the state, school district, community, etc., levels in order to achieve the goals of the equity-based legal action.

Metaphors and Myths Have Shaped American Schools

24. Note some instances when you received benefits for something you may have "deserved" but did not necessarily "earn." Do you believe that "merit" can be passed from parent to child—such as when a person claims to deserve optimal schooling opportunities because "my parents worked hard to raise me right and give me a good education"?

25. "Privileged" may be defined as possessing special opportunities that not everyone has. Perhaps this explains why, in a democracy, it is not a label that people wear comfortably when it refers to advantages that we think we ought to earn rather than something we are born with. How can being middle class or wealthy or going to a fine school be described as privileges? How is it the same or different to say that one is privileged to have nice parents or to live in the United States? How can simply being white or male privilege members of these groups?

26. Sometimes those enterprises that are most highly organized for efficiency seem to waste the most time and treat people who depend on them with the least dignity. Describe the details of some bureaucratic enterprise with which you are familiar, and discuss how its quest for scientific, rational, or efficient organization relates to its fulfilling, or not fulfilling, its central purpose.

27. In your observations of school administrators—or even teachers—you may have noticed some who seem to pattern themselves after corporate business executives and others who seem to be more like teachers. Describe the corporate model of a school administrator. Try to avoid a caricature (cartoonlike portrayal) by providing specific situations and details.

28. *Only a Teacher*. The trend for women to act and be treated according to traditional female stereotypes is much diminished in today's schools, but it still continues. What teaching and administrative practices have you noticed that indicate that gender stereotypes persist in schools? Several segments in the second video in the *Only a Teacher* series: *Those Who Can . . . Teach* ("Those who Can Teach," "The Crusade to Educate Teachers," "The Teacher's Calling," and "The Fight for Teachers' Rights") provide concrete images of how the role of women has evolved in the teaching profession. View and discuss these.

29. Have you ever encountered people who treated complex human problems as if they were "technical puzzles that could be figured out one piece at a time"? Describe the nature of the problem, the person's (or organization's) style and procedures, and the resolution or consequences of that approach

30. The authors contend that consistently, schools have tried to economically spot-fix or target specific school deficits without wasting money on "things that couldn't be proven to raise test scores" (p. 25). Given the national trend emphasizing high-stakes testing, schools and districts may be even more

inclined to address problems in this way. Describe an alternative to high-stakes testing that might in the long run be more effective in improving schools

31. Marketplace competition continues to be at the center of many of today's school reform proposals. Usually, some version of competition is included or implied in discussions of school vouchers, charter schools, and teachers' merit pay, to name just a few current suggestions for school improvement. Read one or more such proposals and/or interview proponents of these changes. Detail their arguments that the changes will increase competition and therefore improve student performance. What criticisms do opponents to these proposals offer?

Hope and Struggle in a Postmodern World

32. Select a particular schooling dilemma, such as a school in which many students do not learn to read well, or a school in which the achievement of students of color is consistently below that of white students. Debate, role play, or construct parallel proposals addressing the dilemma from two different perspectives: (1) a person who subscribes to an ideology of progress, and (2) a person who holds an ideology of hope and struggle.

33. Consider: Cornel West advocates a "critical temper" that "keeps track of social misery, solicits and channels moral outrage to alleviate it, and projects a future in which the potentialities of ordinary people flourish and flower." What actions might a person with such an awareness take in schools? Might not some schools consider a person with such qualities and habits to be a troublemaker? Is it possible to be

critical of the culture and at the same time be accepted by it, or even be seen as a leader in it? What personal qualities, knowledge, personal history, and skills might be needed by a person who is going to be guided by a critical temper in his or her work in schools?

34. Discuss why you think that West and Freire (and first-year teachers Mary Ann Pacheco and Sarine Gureghian) urge educators to focus on their participation in democratic processes, rather than insisting on particular practices that they (West and Freire) have found to be practical or liberating.

WEB SITES

You can link directly to all of the Web sites listed below from the *Teaching to Change the World* Web site located at www.mhhe.com/oakes2e. We recommend linking from that site, as URLs are subject to change and we will be posting updates there.

- **http://www.socsci.kun.nl/ped/whp/histeduc/re adme.html**—A very nicely done international collection of materials, including classic educational books online, newsgroups, and Web links related to the **history of education**.
- **http://www.theatlantic.com/atlantic/issues/95 sep/ets/gsortind.htm**—A series of articles published in the *Atlantic* magazine on **testing and meritocracy** in America from 1896 to 1980. Simply type the words "testing and meritocracy" in the search box for a wealth of information.

- http://bamn.com/resources/97-deeping-seg.htm—Includes the introduction to *Deepening Segregation in American Public Schools* by **Gary Orfield**, Harvard University, and Mark D. Bachmeier, David R. James, and Tamela Eide, Indiana University, that reports the recent research by the Harvard Project on School Desegregation.
- http://www.mecca.org/~crights/brown.html—Exhibit from National Civil Rights Museum on ***Brown v. Board of Education***, with useful link to National Civil Rights Museum.
- http://www.uscharterschools.org—Comprehensive, accessible page with extensive resources and links about **charter school reform**.
- http://www.baylor.edu/~Scott_Moore/West_info.html—Personal Web site with many links (to sites and articles) about **Cornel West**, racial/ethnic issues.
- http://www.americanpromise.com—A companion site for the **PBS series** *American Promise*. Focuses on stories of individuals who have confronted democratic/civil/moral challenges. Includes a teaching guide with general information and particular subject areas, as well as a Teachers' Discussion Forum. Filled with pragmatic, inspiring stories, this site is worth exploring with a critical view of the modernist ideology that undergirds the hope and "promise" under discussion. Sponsored by Farmers Insurance Group.

THE *ONLY A TEACHER* VIDEO SERIES

Relevant Video Segments:

A Teacher Affects Eternity **(Video 1)**
"A Teacher Affects Eternity" (5:00–19:15)
"Saving Souls" (27:00–35:00)
"Assimilating the Alien" (40:00)

Those Who Can . . . Teach **(Video 2)**
"Those who Can Teach" (5:50)
"The Crusade to Educate Teachers" (14:10–18:50)
"The Teacher's Calling" ((23:56–28:42)
"The Fight for Teachers' Rights" (28:42–32:06)

VIDEO REFERENCES

17

CHAPTER 2
TRADITIONAL LEARNING
THEORIES: TRANSMISSION,
TRAINING, AND IQ

OVERVIEW

Chapters 2 and 3 explore theories of learning in their historical, philosophical, and social contexts. These contexts matter because humans quickly shape "scientific" findings to conform to prevailing social beliefs. Our cultural and scientific heritage inclines us toward unproductive—frequently racist—psychological theory, leaving little room for the hopeful and accurate theories that would allow schools to teach well and equitably. The challenge here is twofold: First, teachers need a critique of traditional psychology to help them examine school practices and to scour their common sense for naive or destructive theories that govern learning—particularly conceptions of intelligence. This is primarily the intent of Chapter 2.   Reaching back to the European Enlightenment, we examine the hallmarks of belief that set the philosophical stage for the next three hundred years of Western thought. The second part of the challenge is to understand the nineteenth century attempts to study human behavior scientifically and how they gave rise to the twentieth-century emphasis on laboratory experimentation and scientific testing and measurement. These trends gave rise to flawed science and have had profoundly undemocratic schooling and social consequences.

CHAPTER HEADINGS

GENERATIVE QUESTIONS AND ACTIVITIES

Traditional Learning Theories: *Transmission, Training, and IQ*

1. Recall the people in your life—in school or out—who have made you believe that you were a smart person or clever child. Conversely, recall those people or situations that lowered your estimation of your intelligence. To the degree you can, provide detailed narratives and summaries of these conversations and situations.

***The Bell Curve*: Debates Rage about Intelligence and Learning**

2. Brainstorm on your own or with others some intelligence stereotypes associated with race, religion, or ethnicity. Make the items as "fine grained" as possible: for example, Unitarians, Episcopalians, and

Baptists; Caribbean blacks and blacks from the southern United States; Philippine, Samoan, Hawaiian; Jews from northern Europe and Jews from southern Europe and North Africa; Japanese, Chinese, Thai, Hmong, and so on. Identify commonalities among high-intelligence stereotypes and among low-intelligence stereotypes. How and why do you think these stereotypes were conceived?

3. Competent teachers develop a wealth of professional teaching practices. Yet, Oakes and Lipton assert, "part of teachers' professional knowledge includes their ability to recognize, articulate, and weigh the theories that underlie their own and others' practice" (p. 44). Do you think that most teachers can articulate the learning theories that support their teaching practices? Is this ability really essential? How often and under what circumstances do you suppose teachers are asked to explain learning theories?

4. First-year teacher Cindy Kauionalani Bell explains how sociocultural theorist Luis Moll impacts the way she thinks about her students (pp. 43–44). Summarize how this theory leads to different kinds of learning experiences for students. What advice would you give to a teacher who holds similar beliefs but who works in a traditional school that emphasizes students' deficits? How might an individual teacher be an agent of change in such a school? What type of support might she or he need to be effective?

Changing Conceptions of Learning

5. Intelligence is an important, even central concept in education, schools, and society. Yet, there are astonishingly diverse and often contradictory views of

what intelligence is. Ask a number of people to define what it means to be intelligent. In particular, ask people associated with schooling: students in education courses, graduate students in education, teachers, school administrators, school board members and other education policymakers, and parents—particularly those active in school matters such as members of booster groups and support groups for gifted students.

6. Design a survey question similar to the one above, only this time probe what people think about *knowledge*. You might vary the question to get at what different people think is "useful" knowledge, or what knowledge should make its way into the school and university *canon*.

7. Ask the following question of a variety of people. Follow up by asking them to explain their reasons. Bring this information back to class for analysis.
   To what degree do you think intelligence is inherited?
   - Not at all.
   - A small and insignificant degree.
   - A small but significant degree.
   - Enough to explain important intelligence differences.
   - Enough to be the most important factor in determining intelligence.

8. Reification—making abstractions into something concrete and real—is such a common practice that we can only hope to be aware of it, not really to eliminate it. However, social scientists such as teachers have a special responsibility to be careful with this informal

language use. Listen carefully for, and record, examples of reification that might otherwise have escaped your notice. Here are a few examples: "society says" (instead of pointing to particular norms or laws that compel people to conform), "she's an A student" (instead of referring to her grade point average), "the honors kids" (instead of students enrolled in honors classes).

The Promise of Scientific Schooling
Intelligence, Learning, and Merit: You Get What You Deserve

9. If your IQ were tested to be 100, what would be your response? Explain how or why this would this be pleasing to you or disappointing.

10. Many argue that standardized tests stem from the IQ tests designed in the early twentieth century. Review criticisms of the early IQ tests. (Try searching "early IQ tests" on the Internet for starters.) Do the tests seem objective and fair to you? Why might the tests be prone to cultural or racial bias? Provide examples.

11. Currently, many are touting high-stakes testing as an effective way to increase students' academic performance, especially in low-performing schools. Their advocacy of tests is typically based on a *theory* of why such tests "work." Discuss elements of this theory. (Hints: public disclosure of test scores will embarrass and thus motivate low-performing schools to do better; teachers will use the tests to diagnose specific learning gaps or needs in individual students and then address those needs; students who fear being held back will try harder; schools will operate more efficiently if students must be certified by the tests as being prepared before entering the next grade or graduating.) Search for other

23

supports marshaled in defense of high-stakes tests. Given what you know about standardized tests and schools, do you believe these to be well-founded reasons? Stage a debate in which half of the students present reasons for high-stakes tests and the other half argue against them.

12. People often make informal judgments about one another's intelligence. Wouldn't it be better—more accurate—if people just made their tested intelligence public? Try writing a short story or skit that explores events and relationships when a small community or school decides that everyone will wear their IQs on a button fastened to their clothing.

Learning as Behavioral Training
Schooling as Behavioral Training

13. One of the best ways to understand behavioral principles is through the methods of an expert dog trainer. Such a trainer does not expect the dog to "understand" or make sense of instructions; instead, the trainer follows a strict regime of conditioning. Look through one or more puppy/dog training books, videos, or Internet sites and discuss how dogs' learning abilities might be different from those of humans. Revisit this "exercise" after reading Chapter 3.

14. Reflect on your own K-12 schooling and some of the "systems" or routines your own teachers used to motivate students to behave correctly. Comment on how well they seemed to work for the students and the teachers. Were these routines consistently applied within particular classrooms? Across the school? How did you feel and respond while learning under these conditions?

15. Throughout their book, Oakes and Lipton associate behavioral learning approaches with conservative social and political views. They reinforce this argument in later chapters, but do you think, at this point in the book, that such an association is valid? Or, on the other hand, could you argue that this might be a "slanted," biased, or unsupportable view—perhaps designed to discredit behaviorism or conservative political, social, and educational views?

The Limits of Transmission and Training

16. Along with the authors, first-year teacher Dung Bich Lam suggests that a behavioral learning approach may be harmful to his students. Although you have not necessarily been introduced to alternative learning theories at this point, intuitively generate ideas for different models of learning and behavior management. How might your own theories do a better job of supporting the needs of culturally and linguistically diverse students than behavioral approaches?

17. Observe an elementary or secondary school classroom (an alternative would be a college classroom; another alternative would be to observe a family's interactions over a period of several hours) and identify all the cases you can in which rewards and punishments are used. Rewards might include tangible items such as treats or grades, or intangible ones such as recognition or approval. (You might preface this exercise by brainstorming of all the types of rewards and punishments one might expect to find, and then challenging students to find actual cases of these as well as unanticipated rewards and punishments.)

18. Take a street-corner poll about learning (e.g., outside a grocery store, the post office, or other site where you'll find a cross-section of residents.) Tell passersby that you are a university student studying how people think about learning. Ask them to explain to you how human beings learn. Gather 10–15 responses. Decide how they match (or don't) the learning theories presented in this chapter and the next.

WEB SITES

- You can link directly to all of the Web sites listed below from the *Teaching to Change the World* Web site located at www.mhhe.com/oakes2e. We recommend linking from that site, as URLs are subject to change and we will be posting updates there.

- **http://www.morehead-st.edu/people/w.willis/romantics.html**—"Major Themes in the Educational Thought of Rousseau." Also related to Johann Pestalozzi.

- **http://www.mindbodysoul.com/corpus/mind/iq/memory/investigate/main.html**—"Investigating the I.Q. Test." A fun, somewhat interactive site related to **Alfred Binet and IQ.**

- **http://tiger.coe.missouri.edu/~t377/btheorists.html**—"Theorists of Behaviorism" and "Behaviorist's Diner" offer brief descriptions of the theorists who promote behaviorism as well as providing examples of assessment and management strategies guided by behaviorist principles.

- **http://www.edletter.org/past/issues/1999-ma/human.shtml**—This back issue of the *Harvard Educational Letter* features an article entitled "The

Human Cost of Over-Reliance on Tests," by Adria Steinberg.

- **http://www.mugu.com/cgi-bin/Upstream/People/Murray/bc-crit.html**— Charles Murray's lengthy, inflammatory response to critics of *The Bell Curve*. Article is manipulatively written and betrays an obvious political bias. Could be good for inciting discussion!

CHAPTER 3
CONTEMPORARY LEARNING THEORIES: PROBLEM SOLVING AND UNDERSTANDING

OVERVIEW

Chapter 3, "Contemporary Learning Theories: Problem Solving and Understanding," turns to the second challenge presented by the discipline of psychology: to explore emerging theories that permit and direct us to equitable teaching. The most educationally relevant of these theories weave together knowledge from social science theory and research including sociology, anthropology, psychology, and education. Recent advances in these fields present learning as something that each learner must actively construct. We contrast this constructivist view with earlier theories that knowledge is absolute. We take a related view of intelligence, emphasizing that it is both social and constructed. Each of these newer views is well supported by theory and research, and each supports the social-justice goal of using and respecting the knowledge, language, and cultures of diverse groups of students.

CHAPTER HEADINGS

GENERATIVE QUESTIONS AND ACTIVITIES

Contemporary Learning Theories: *Problem Solving and Understanding*

1. Many essentially "educational" questions—questions about learning—are also political questions. Public discussion of these professional matters is included in the editorial and political sections of the newspaper as often as in the "features" sections. Keep a file of newspaper articles about local political/educational issues—paying special attention to how the discussion reflects particular perceptions of how people learn. Note also whether particular perceptions of learning tend to align with particular views of how schools should operate.

Learning as Thinking and Understanding

2. Consider a body of knowledge (a special interest) that you have, or a particular well-developed skill (a sport, line of work, or profession). Think about how you learned it. Did you come to have this knowledge or skill in a spiraling fashion rather than a strict, linear, adding-on of additional knowledge or skill? If so, trace that process.

3. Keep a record of your own schooling experiences for one week. Note what you are "supposed" to learn at several levels—that is, in outline fashion, the broad topics and subtopics. Identify whether you are expected (1) to learn by solving problems or (2) in Dewey's terms, to learn by "rehearsing second-hand information or by memorizing for the sake of producing correct replies at the proper time." Allow for the possibility that

both approaches will be important, and if they are, discuss their relationship and relative importance.

4. Oakes and Lipton offer some examples of Piaget's concepts of assimilation and accommodation. (They ask the reader to distinguish between the questions: "What did you learn about the Civil War?" and "How do you understand the Civil War differently?" They describe getting used to driving a car in England under very different circumstances than driving in America—pp. 73–74.) Working alone or with others, construct additional examples of schooling and everyday learning that help to distinguish assimilation and accommodation, while using these concepts to identify the dynamic processes of disequilibrium and equilibration.

The Cognitive "Revolution"

5. Unlike many textbooks, *Teaching to Change the World* does not provide a glossary that gives dictionary-like definitions for the technical terms the authors use. For example, at one point they write, "This . . . is probably what most people experience as 'motivation,'" rather than defining the term. Why do you suppose they take this approach? Finally, construct your own definition of motivation—using Oakes and Lipton's discussion, a dictionary and other sources, your own examples, and the help and questions of others.

6. How might the knowledge of Bruner's spiral curriculum along with an awareness of developmental stages affect a teacher's lesson planning? Conversely, how might a lack of knowledge of these concepts diminish the effectiveness of a teacher's lessons?

7. In this chapter Oakes and Lipton favor sociocultural views of learning that differ considerably from how most schools and teachers have approached learning in the past. Much of the remaining book offers further support for sociocultural theory. Do you anticipate that these views will become "mainstream" views, and that within the first quarter of the twenty-first century persuasive arguments will have altered the way most teachers teach? Explain why you do or do not think so.

8. Oakes and Lipton use some of the language popular with many of today's cultural theorists, including the phrase "dominant culture." Some people take offense at this term, protesting that they, personally, do not intend to and do not in fact impose their culture on others. Yet, if you are white and middle class, you are likely a member of this dominant culture. Are you comfortable with this term or idea? How do you defend its use or argue against it?

9. Describe the details of a recent learning experience (in or out of school) in which a more knowledgeable person guided you to understanding by asking questions or providing information that was within your Zone of Proximal Development (ZPD).

10. As part of their discussion of the Zone of Proximal Development, the authors describe scaffolding as providing students with the temporary support to perform at a level they would be unable to reach independently. Teachers Cindy Kauionalani Bell (pp. 88 and 92) and Benjamin Chang (p. 93) provide examples of different forms of scaffolding such as instructional conversation, heterogeneous cooperative

grouping, and contextualizing learning in students' life experiences. Given these examples, design your own lesson plan in which you explicitly describe the form of scaffolding you will employ. Remember, you do not need to use the same types as those described by the new teachers in this book.

11. Think about the classroom in which you are student teaching or observing. Over a period of days, keep a record of the guiding teacher's scaffolding the students. Has the scaffolding proven effective? If so, how?

12. Describe—in detail—how you learned a body of knowledge through an apprenticeship relationship. How did this affect your identity? For example, a person might identify himself as a cook in part because he has helped, watched, and been given appropriate tasks by an older person who is an accomplished cook.

13. Is there a person in your family who is baffled by the kind of knowledge you are gaining in college? Are you sometimes baffled yourself? What other schooling experiences have you had in which the school's knowledge did not match well with the kind of knowledge some members of your family understood or valued? Or, if your family culture is very compatible with American schooling, interview others who might have to accommodate the valued knowledge of two cultures.

14. Consider a young child you know whom you have always considered very smart. Why, specifically, do you think this is the case? What are the specific behaviors that make you think this child is smart? (For example, the child has a large vocabulary.) Are all of these behaviors consistent with your own cultural

33

values? (For example, if you see a talkative child as intelligent, that may be consistent with your belief that intelligent people have an extensive vocabulary.)

Why *Do* Children Learn?

15. The simple folk expression "two heads are better than one" contains the seed of the idea of distributed intelligence. With this in mind, describe how a highly competitive culture might actually lower the culture's distributed intelligence. Recall a time when competition among individuals produced a less satisfactory result than if several members of a family or group had been able to collaborate, taking advantage of their combined knowledge and problem-solving capacities. Review news articles and features that discuss the biographies, activities, and concerns of school-aged young people. In each case, write a few speculative sentences about that young person's probable identity or identities. Then project the possible impact that that identity would have on the person's schooling. You will likely have to go beyond the "evidence" in the article—you might even risk exposing some of your own stereotypes. For example, "The seventeen-year-old in this article is a 4-H club member. She sees herself as a hard-working teenager who is extraordinarily responsible. She is not given to theoretical musings unless she sees an immediate practical application. If I were her high school counselor, I might encourage her to take chemistry rather than a fourth year of foreign language." Note, as in this example, and as is explored in several chapters in the book, that identities are "negotiated" in the culture. One can hardly hold on to an identity unless peers and important others agree that the identity "fits" and share what it means to hold that identity. Thus, identities for gang members, athletes,

scholars, and so on depend, to some degree, on shared cultural perceptions—often stereotypes.

Cognition, Culture, and Teaching to Change the World

16. Throughout the chapter, the authors assert that intelligence is socially constructed. As a teacher, you will face the challenge of disrupting the myth that intelligence is inherited and innate. Your students, especially (but not only) older students, will have been influenced by this misconception and may agree with it in regard to themselves and their classmates. What might you do to prepare your students to cope with or struggle against these attitudes both within and outside of your classroom? Do you think school is the appropriate place for this type of discussion?

WEB SITES

You can link directly to all of the Web sites listed below from the *Teaching to Change the World* Web site located at www.mhhe.com/oakes2e. We recommend linking from that site, as URLs are subject to change and we will be posting updates there.

- http://lrs.ed.uiuc.edu/students/janicke/Dewey.html —Provides a brief biography of John Dewey and a partial bibliography. Tells how to join the Internet discussion group "Dewey-L."
- http://www.piaget.org—**Jean Piaget Society** —An extensive site that includes suggested reading for students.

- **http://www.newhorizons.org/trm_gardner.html** —Information about Howard Gardner's theory of **multiple intelligences.**

- **http://pzweb.harvard.edu/default.htm**—Howard Gardner, David Perkins, and multiple intelligences on **Harvard's Project Zero** home page. The Harvard Project Zero research group at Harvard Graduate School of Education investigates development of learning processes. "Project Zero's mission is to understand and enhance learning, thinking and creativity in the arts and other disciplines for individuals and institutions." Many resources, materials.

- **http://www.funderstanding.com/theories1.html** —Concise information about ten major **learning theories.**

- **http://www.uwsp.edu/acad/educ/lwilson/LEARN ING**—Information about **learning theories** and resources.

- **http://www.kolar.org/vygotsky**—Provides a comprehensive list of "Vygotsky Resources" with links for biographical information, sociocultural learning theories, information for teachers, and other resources.

- **http://www.crede.ucsc.edu/** UCSC's Center for Research on Education, Diversity & Excellence (CREDE). Their home page offers links for research and resources that are aligned with sociocultural learning theory.

CHAPTER 4
CURRICULUM: PHILOSOPHY, HISTORY, AND POLITICS: WHAT SHOULD STUDENTS LEARN?

OVERVIEW

Chapter 4, "Curriculum: Philosophy, History, and Politics: What Should Students Learn?" looks beneath the superficial consensus that all children need reading and writing, mathematics, science, and whatever else it takes to be responsible citizens. Like everything else about schools, the American curriculum is deeply rooted in history and politics, as well as in the intrinsic human eagerness to learn. Debates about what content best serves students and society and how teachers should organize and present that content reflect starkly different views of the nature of knowledge, the nature of humans, and the nature of a good society. Today, fierce political battles overwhelm professional curriculum debates. Political conservatives argue that schools must continue to transmit traditional knowledge, while political progressives assert that schools must reflect the multiple American cultural and linguistic traditions. Chapter 4 reviews these issues and sets the stage for the current controversies over local and national "standards" in the school subjects.

CHAPTER HEADINGS

GENERATIVE QUESTIONS AND ACTIVITIES

Philosophies of Education: Some Basics

1. Oftentimes, poor students of color and more affluent
   white students are exposed to different curricular
   programs that reflect different educational philosophies.
   In other words, some people or schools may hold
   different educational philosophies *because* they apply
   the philosophies to different groups of students. Think
   about schools with which you are familiar and comment
   on whether the schools' or teachers' educational
   philosophies seem to be aligned with particular groups
   of students. This investigation can occur within a single
   school that serves different groups or across two or
   more schools.

2. Although some argue that students' diverse needs require different curricula, others contend that by addressing different learning needs schools can help nearly all students master the same curriculum. Stated simply, and perhaps oversimplifying, should schools teach different students differently with the goal that all students will learn the same curriculum? Or should schools teach all students in pretty much the same way, assuming that they can all be successful by learning different curricula that are suited to their skills and capacities?

Why Do We Have to Learn This? Traditions and Debates

3. Recall a class or "unit" from your own elementary, secondary, or college education. At some point you might have assumed that the class was built around "pure" facts and knowledge, but now consider how the political and cultural dimensions of knowledge and education were very likely interwoven with the knowledge and skills presented. Begin by asking critical questions such as "Why this particular content emphasis?" "Why are these particular students enrolled?" "Are there particular students whose participation and whose prior experiences the course or teacher seems to favor?" "What legitimate information or theories are not included?" "Are there neglected opportunities to consider socially relevant applications of the knowledge?" With a specific class in mind, what additional critical questions can you think of asking?

4. In this chapter, as with several others, Oakes and Lipton infuse some history of education as background for the issues under discussion. However, it is important to keep in mind that this is not primarily a text on the

history of education, and a professional educator will want to explore and study much more of the history and politics of the field. Why is it important for professionals—educators, scientists, lawyers, journalists, and so on—to have a knowledge of the historical context of their field? Why, for example, is such knowledge necessary to teach mathematics to fifteen-year-olds or teach six-year-olds to read?

5. Oakes and Lipton state, "People of greater wealth and status saw their own well-being enhanced by common schools, even if their children did not attend them. Everyone would benefit, they reasoned, if schools could turn out productive workers and good citizens." The authors suggest that social elites often support common, public schools with their own security and prosperity in mind more than the well-being of those who are less privileged. Do you think that the authors are realistic, or overly cynical? What evidence would you use to defend your position?

6. *Only a Teacher*. The first portion of the video *A Teacher Affects Eternity* portrays the emergence of the common school, standardized curriculum, and the resulting feminization of the teaching force. In addition, several segments from the second video in the series, *Those Who Can . . . Teach*, make these connections ("Those Who Can Teach," The Crusade to Educate Teachers," and "Teaching in the Education Factory"). How are these three trends tied together? Does your analysis apply similarly to current conditions that favor standardization and a teaching force that is predominantly composed of women? How might recent economic and demographic trends continue or change the traditional makeup of the teaching workforce?

7. Some sectors of contemporary society claim that today's public schools lack opportunities for students to learn "traditional" religious or moral values. People with these views often attribute the existence of many social problems to this omission. What do you think of the religious content in McGuffey's and Webster's textbooks along with their moral and religious underpinning of middle-class prosperity? Are there comparable inclusions (or intrusions) of religious and moral content in today's schools that may escape notice because they do not seem as old-fashioned and heavy-handed as McGuffey's and Webster's?

8. ***Only a Teacher***. Several segments from the PBS video *A Teacher Affects Eternity* ("A Higher Standard of Deportment" and "Teaching: It's Not All Academic") claim that teaching is an identity more than a profession. A central part of this identity is being a force of moral and social good as well as a community leader who sets an example for all members of society. This has always been a heavy responsibility and challenge for teachers. What special challenges and obstacles would a social-justice teacher face both in living up to existing standards and in establishing new ones? Try to create or report realistic examples.

9. Why is "hands-on" or experience-based learning likely to be more compatible with sociocultural theories of learning than traditional teacher-centered or teacher-directed lessons? Compare two lessons you experienced or observed, selecting one because it involved students in active participation and the other because it emphasized "pencil and paper" and listening and responding. Elaborate on the relative advantages to you, your comfort with the format, and the ease or difficulty the teacher likely had in preparing the lessons.

10. Review Oakes and Lipton's comparison of Dewey to other progressive reformers. Describe one of your own student experiences with (or a recent observation of) teaching that sought to "develop in students a character that would build democratic and interdependent communities." What was your reaction to this experience? If you did not experience or witness such lessons, select a lesson (perhaps a "near miss") in which the teacher missed the opportunity to develop such "character." What might the teacher have done differently?

The Struggle for a Twenty-First-Century Curriculum

11. Oakes and Lipton offer Lauren Resnick's model of nine elements of higher-order thinking as important considerations for designing lessons—that is, these elements enhance students' opportunities to learn by finding meaning, applying multiple criteria, exerting effort, feeling in charge of their own problem solving, and so on. (Caution! Someone else might find seven or fifteen!) Focus on a particular lesson you have observed or experienced. Which, if any, of these elements were present? How might the teacher have designed the lesson differently if his goal was for the learners to internalize these elements of higher-order thinking so they become characteristics of the learners themselves? In other words, how might this teacher have used the lesson as an opportunity to nurture the critical-thinking habit of "finding structure in apparent disorder," so that students would bring it to *all* learning situations?

12. Consider one of your own school assignments, class problems, or another problem that has been presented as calling for an unambiguous, straightforward solution *or a single, limited, and "correct" answer.* What

additional insights into the problem might you gain by considering that assignment or problem in light of Resnick's elements of "higher-order thinking"?

13. There has been a new round of calls for schools to assume many of the functions of Jane Addams' settlement houses earlier in the century. If schools were to become more like community centers serving the combined social, educational, health, employment, and cultural needs of the community, what might be some of the social and educational advantages? What are some likely criticisms of schools assuming this broader role? Search out and describe a school in your own or a nearby community that is making such attempts. (Note that these efforts are not always official school policy, but may be infused within a particular school culture. In some cases, the school may not see itself as doing anything extraordinary, but simply serving its students and their families.) Also, take a close look at a community-service agency or center and describe the extent of its school-related services. Interview personnel at a community agency and ask them, in particular, whether and how their agency and local schools could work more closely together.

14. Oakes and Lipton clearly agree with W. E. B. DuBois's words, "We should fight to the last ditch to keep open the right to learn, the right to have examined in our schools not only what we believe, not only what our leaders say, but what the leaders of other groups and nations, and the leaders of other centuries have said." On the other hand, critics of this view, such as Alan Bloom, believe that leaders of other groups and nations who promote *their* beliefs create unhealthy tensions and divisions in the culture, and as Americans we should remain focused on *our* beliefs. Defend one side or

another in this dispute; or discuss/explore your indecision.

15. The authors caution teachers against providing their students with a tokenized version of multicultural education—one that does "little more than mention the 'place' of minorities and immigrants in the unquestioned story and content of American culture" (p. 129). How can you avoid this limited representation of people of color and other minority groups? How can you address issues that a more "typical" multicultural curriculum would miss, such as institutionalized racism and other oppressive social structures? With a partner or group, review and analyze a single week's lessons for a particular class. Brainstorm how you could meet worthwhile curricular (in this case, "subject matter") objectives while at the same time you seamlessly include content that contributes to the class's multicultural needs and composition.

16. In your analysis of the curriculum described in the previous question, discuss major tenets of critical pedagogy (teaching as an inherently political practice, action based on reflection, etc.).

17. Are you at least somewhat fluent in a language other than English? If you were teaching in a school with many children from Spanish-speaking families, would you embark on a program to learn Spanish? Would your answer be different if the students' language were Vietnamese, Armenian, Farsi, or French? Have you ever said or felt, "I'm not good at languages"? Interview someone from a culture where learning two or more languages is considered normal (e.g., many Africans learn both a tribal language and a national language; most Swiss citizens learn at least two

languages). Ask them how difficult they consider learning a second language to be.

18. Interview one or more teachers who are fluent in the language (other than English) that many of their students and parents speak as a first language. Ask them about the advantages of being bilingual or multilingual. Interview one or more teachers who are not fluent speakers of the language spoken by their students or their parents. How do their views and attitudes differ from those of the bilingual teacher?

19. Having good interviewing skills is an invaluable teaching, learning, research, and professional skill. Recall your own opportunities to conduct interviews. Discuss some of your difficulties and successes. Are there courses or resources at your institution that could help you sharpen your interviewing skills? Select a subject that you might teach some day, and discuss how interviewing skills could enhance your students' opportunities in that particular subject if they were to learn such skills and put them into practice.

20. Develop a list of your skills, resources, and background that give you *cultural capital* (try for five items). How are you able to "code switch" in your language, attitude, dress, and the cultural capital that you present to others?

Current Debates about Constructivism and Multiculturalism

21. Explain why a sociocultural view of how people learn encourages developing a multicultural curriculum. Similarly, explain why a behavioral emphasis encourages a monocultural curriculum.

22. In the section entitled "Goals 2000 and the Standards Movement," the authors detail the evolution of academic standards in America's public schools. They contend, "By the mid 1990's, the backlash against cognitively and socioculturally oriented curricula had captured enormous public sympathy and policy clout" (p. 142). Do you see evidence of this trend in the academic standards mandated in your state or local district? Explain. What are the implications for the students with whom you work?

23. Oakes and Lipton argue, "Perhaps the most dramatic example of the battle against 'regressive multiculturalism' has been the 'English for the Children' movement" (p. 144). For example, following the passage of Proposition 227 in 1998, most California public schools effectively eliminated all bilingual programs and primary language instruction. Are bilingual programs in your own locale under similar attack, are they thriving, or are they just holding on? Interview a teacher, administrator, and parent from a school with linguistically diverse students. How do they perceive their current programs—i.e., secure and developing? Under siege? What have been recent trends in outcomes (academic, social, etc.) for students?

A Final Question

24. Oakes and Lipton assert that current debates about curriculum can be traced back to age-old arguments about (a) the nature of reality, (b) humans' ability to "know" it, and (c) what's worth knowing. Apply these three categories to the curriculum debates that may affect the students with whom you (would like to) work. How do the three categories help explain why certain models of curricula may currently be more popular than others?

WEB SITES

You can link directly to all of the Web sites listed below from the *Teaching to Change the World* Web site located at www.mhhe.com/oakes2e. We recommend linking from that site, as URLs are subject to change and we will be posting updates there.

- **http://www.edgateway.net/er101/curr.html**— "Curriculum in Education Reform." Shows some common characteristics of recent **curriculum reforms** and provides useful links.

- **http://www.ed.gov/G2k/doc-stan.html**— Documents about **standards** and supportive of them.

- **http://www.nameorg.org/**—**National Association for Multicultural Education**.

- **http://nlu.nl.edu/ace/Resources/Freire.html**— Biography of and selected bibliography on **Paulo Freire**.

- **http://nlu.nl.edu/ace/Resources/Documents/Freir eIssues.html**—"Issues in Freirean Pedagogy" by Tom Heaney. Covers **Paulo Freire**'s philosophy, critical consciousness, institutionalization, and so on. Especially useful here are links to the glossary.

- **http://www.wmc.edu/academics/library/pub/jcp/j cp.html The Journal of Critical Pedagogy**, an online publication.

- **http://www.perfectfit.org/CT/info.html**—"Rage and Hope" explores critical pedagogy by attempting to answer the question, "Whose future, story, and interests does the school represent?" This site also offers many useful links to the work of important critical theorists such as Paulo Freire, Henry

Giroux, Michael Apple, and Peter McLaren, as well as other references.

- **http://www.usc.edu/dept/education/CUE/—**The home page for the University of Southern California's Center for Urban Education. (SHOULD I KEEP THIS????)

- **http://www.NoChildLeftBehind.gov/—**The "No Child Left Behind" home page.

- **http://www.education-world.com/standards—** "Education World" presents the objectives of the voluntary National Education Standards for the major subject areas; it also provides links to the state standards as well as to educational articles and specific subject resources.

THE *ONLY A TEACHER* VIDEO SERIES

Relevant Video Segments:

A Teacher Affects Eternity **(Video 1)**
"A Higher Standard of Deportment" (19:20–23:38)
"Teaching: It's Not All Academic" (23:38–27:00)

Those Who Can . . . Teach **(Video 2)**
"Those Who Can Teach" (5:50)
"The Crusade to Educate Teachers" (14:10–18:50)
"Teaching in the Education Factory" (32:06–45:20)

CHAPTER 5
CURRICULUM: THE SUBJECT MATTERS

OVERVIEW

Chapter 5, "Curriculum: The Subject Matters," spells out how the professional and political curriculum debates surface in four major academic content areas, shaping what and how students learn in each. The standards movement has brought discussions of exactly what math, language arts, science, and social studies students should learn into the political arena. One side—political liberals, social progressives, and most experts on teaching the subjects—argues that a socially just curriculum gives every child access to the most important ideas of the core disciplines. This happens, they contend, when teachers emphasize meaning-making and understanding and recognize that facts and skills can best be learned in the context of these important core ideas. The other side—political conservatives, traditionalists, and some scholars in the subject areas—focuses first on the mastery of basic facts and skills. They insist that basic facts and skills are prerequisite to complex ideas. These disputes have been intense: they are often called history, science, math, and phonics "wars" as they are fought by local school boards and state and national policymaking bodies.

CHAPTER HEADINGS

GENERATIVE QUESTIONS AND ACTIVITIES

What Knowledge? Whose Knowledge? Knowledge for Whom?

1. As background for this chapter and for the questions that follow, take a look at a few "curriculum guides" used by different grade levels, for different subjects, in different schools. When you can, interview teachers or administrators to get a sense of whether and how these guides reflect what these educators think is their most important work. Look for evidence in the guides— particular items and language or terms used to express them—showing whether sociocultural perspectives are thought to be important in the school or district

Mathematics

2. Briefly sketch the history of your mathematics coursework. Would you identify yourself as highly competent, not very competent, or somewhere in between? Did you take calculus in high school? Why or why not? Once you graduated from high school, was a college major in mathematics, the sciences, or engineering a realistic choice for you if you had an interest in these career areas? In your estimation, does it take special talents to acquire skill in mathematics? Recount instances when someone skilled in mathematics lavished encouragement on you to study math. Describe the circumstances of your meeting— perhaps a guest speaker in a mathematics class, or a woman engineer, mathematician, or scientist. Did you ever have an African American mathematics teacher? What was the racial and gender composition of your "advanced" high school mathematics classes? Ask a variety of K-12 students, "What does it take to be good

at math?" Share and analyze these questions and answers, along with others that may arise.

3. Is the discussion of progressive views of mathematics learning in this chapter consistent with your prior understanding of math learning? Or have you always assumed that traditional approaches were the "only" way? Do you think your math learning—both knowledge and appreciation of mathematics—might have been different if you had had progressive mathematics teachers in elementary and high school? On the other hand, not all progressive approaches in mathematics education are necessarily carried out competently. Describe your best and worst math class experiences—whether traditionally or progressively taught.

4. Does a teacher need a very thorough understanding of mathematics to do a good job of teaching math to elementary school children? Explain your answer.

5. First-year teacher Zeba Palomino (pp. 157–158) describes her "critical" approach to teaching high school mathematics. Many of her ideas reflect the constructivist and student-centered philosophy posited in *Everybody Counts*. Discuss the degree to which Palomino's discussion applies equally well to younger students in elementary school.

6. Why is it important for all adults in a school to have a high degree of mathematics competence? (Or why is that a foolish proposition?) How would a teacher of English, art, social studies, or another subject be able to offer enhanced learning opportunities if she or he had extensive mathematics knowledge and math-teaching

competencies (although not necessarily all the professional skills of a trained math teacher)?

7. Oakes and Lipton argue that "pedagogical strategies must reach out to African Americans and Latinos, groups that have been underrepresented in mathematics. Special efforts must be undertaken to respond to the fact that girls, whose participation in advanced math courses equals and often surpasses that of boys, are still underrepresented in mathematics, engineering and other math-intensive careers" (p. 160). Based on what you know of traditional and contemporary learning theories (see Chapters 2 and 3), what types of pedagogical approaches do you think the authors advocate? Why do you think these approaches would be effective for African Americans, Latinos, and girls from all racial groups?

8. Using your answer to number 7 as a guide, design a math lesson plan that employs a culturally relevant and gender-sensitive pedagogical approach for the grade you (would like to) teach. How would you strategically go about teaching such a lesson, given the fact that the current mathematical standards focus heavily on rote computation? (Secondary teachers, do not "excuse" yourself from this question with the claim that you are not a math teacher. Reflect critically on your own math classes and discuss instances of cultural and gender relevance and sensitivity. Also, discuss how the teacher might have made a particular lesson more relevant and sensitive.)

English Language Arts

9. Reflecting on your own English language arts background, rank, in order of importance, the areas you

wish you had more extensive opportunities to learn: grammar and spelling, expository composition, narrative/fiction writing, reading for comprehension, literature, research, and any other opportunities. Explain why you wish you had more opportunities for some and why you ranked others lower.

10. Has reading fiction broadened your cultural horizons? List those novels that have opened your eyes and heart to peoples of different cultures, backgrounds, ethnicities, and so on. In particular, list the novels you have read by African American, Latino/Hispanic, Asian, or non-American, nonwhite authors. Select one or more to comment on specifically, and comment on your overall experience reading (or not reading) these works. Were any of these works assigned in school? If not, who, if anybody, suggested that you read them?

11. Oakes and Lipton advocate a "Balanced Literacy Approach," meaning a literacy program that emphasizes both phonics instruction (phonemic awareness) and a whole language approach. One reason to implement such an approach is that a wealth of research demonstrates that teaching discrete skills in a meaningful context is more effective than teaching them in isolation. However, there is an ever-growing trend to adopt "scripted" language arts programs, especially in "underperforming" districts that tend to serve low-income students of color and English learners. Such programs do not support this balanced model. Should social-justice educators accept or resist these "scripted" programs? Explain your opinion. You may want to use first-year teacher Benji Chang's account of such a situation (pp. 177–178) to guide your thinking.

12. In part because of their schooling experiences, many people do not begin reading high-quality, culturally relevant fiction until *after* they stop going to school. Project yourself ten years into the future. Do you see yourself as an avid or frequent reader of fiction? What other avenues do you expect you will follow in the arts and literature, in your living and working circumstances, in academic reading and study, and so on, that will keep you in engaged in multicultural experiences.

13. Oakes and Lipton continue to emphasize the political influences on determining what is legitimately taught in school. Interview one or more teachers and ask how their curriculum decisions are influenced by the political climate in their community or state. Probe for specific short-term effects that result from recent legislation or school-board policy, as well as long-range influences that teachers notice taking place over many years. Be sure to ask your interviewee to reflect on trends or events that he or she sees as positive. Some teachers develop a perception that they are not affected by circumstances outside their schools or classrooms (in much the same way that a teenager might insist that he is not influenced by styles or fads), With this in mind, be sure to prepare for the interview by having specific knowledge of the political climate and recent events in the teachers' communities or states. This knowledge will help you think of follow-up questions and prompt more complete answers.

Social Studies

14. Conservative educators express concerns that critical multicultural approaches in school, especially as they relate to United States history, cause cultural

divisiveness, pit races and ethnicities against each other, and deny students the factual cultural building blocks a unified nation needs. Have you ever experienced such multicultural pedagogy? What do you think was (or would have been) its effect on you? Was this effect on you the same as its effect on "most other" students?

15. Oakes and Lipton cite these questions from *History on Trial: Culture Wars and the Teaching of the Past:* "Do we revise and reinterpret the past to tell previously ignored stories because they reflect present-day values and speak to the issues of our own time? Or do we believe that the primary role of schools, textbooks, and museums is to preserve traditional versions of the past, to teach the basic facts, and to instill patriotism in our students?" How do you answer these questions?

16. Review the history of oppressed peoples in your locale: Native Americans, African Americans, Asians, Hispanics, and other immigrants and religious groups. How and how extensively are these histories represented to local schoolchildren? What distinctions are made among the experiences of these groups according to their ethnicity—particularly race? What are the lasting or continuing effects of these histories on today's populations? Is there evidence that not all minorities experience similar social or educational effects due to their inclusion or omission—representation or misrepresentation—in texts and schools?

17. Oakes and Lipton cite the social studies standards' distinction between "historical thinking skills" and "historical understandings," but they do not develop these with examples. Select a contemporary "event"

that is likely to have historical significance, and suggest how students in K-12 schools might find the relevance of this event by focusing both their historical thinking skills *and* their historical understandings on the event.

Science

18. Review your K-12 science experiences. Were they largely based on project and laboratory experiences, or were they largely lecture/demonstration/reading/memorizing? Describe a course that gave you important science knowledge, interest, and background. Do you recall any particular passionate science, social, or political interests of the teacher of this course? How were these interests relevant or irrelevant to your own interests?

19. Often, middle and high schools use mathematics background or achievement as a "filter" to screen students they expect to be low achievers out of higher-level science classes. Were your science opportunities influenced (either positively or negatively) by your proficiency in mathematics? Explain/analyze the effects of linking math proficiency to science on your own course-taking and future science interest. How could this linkage have social-justice implications?

20. Oakes and Lipton identify the following four "new" conceptions of science *content* contained within the science standards, calling them "provocative and exciting":
    - The content of science cannot be placed outside of science's unifying concepts and processes.
    - Participation in inquiry is scientific content, not just process.

- Scientific knowledge is not distinct from societal challenges.
- The history of science is science content that underscores science as a human and social enterprise.

These standards are far from what most people are used to thinking of as science content. Select one and offer arguments that might be posed by someone who holds a traditional view of curriculum. Then answer the arguments.

WEB SITES

You can link directly to all of the Web sites listed below from the *Teaching to Change the World* Web site located at www.mhhe.com/oakes2e. We recommend linking from that site, as URLs are subject to change and we will be posting updates there.

- **http://www.ncte.org**—The **National Council of Teachers of English**.
- **http://www.reading.org**—**International Reading Association**.
- **http://www.writingproject.org/**—Home page of the **National Writing Project**.
- **http://www.sscnet.ucla.edu/nchs**—**National Center for History in the Schools**.
- **http://www.ncss.org/**—The **National Council for the Social Studies**.
- **http://www.facing.org/**—**Facing History and Ourselves** connects history to the day-to-day experiences of students by revealing how violence and hate can destroy a society, and how the

decisions of ordinary people shape an age and ultimately history.

- **http://www.nsta.org**—Home page of the **National Science Teachers Association**.

- **http://http://www.oneonta.edu/~baumanpr/ncge/rstf.htm**—**National Council for Geographic Education** at the Indiana University of Pennsylvania.

- **http://www.nctm.org/**—The **National Council of Teachers of Mathematics**.

- **http://www.lhs.berkeley.edu**—**Lawrence Hall of Science at the University of California at Berkeley** offers an exciting collection of hands-on science and math activities and materials.

- **http://www.enc.org/weblinks/science**—ENC, the Eisenhower National Clearinghouse for **science education**, provides an up-to-date list of Web resources related to mathematics and science teaching.

- **http://www.enc.org/weblinks/science**—ENC, the Eisenhower National Clearinghouse for **mathematics education**, provides an up-to-date list of Web resources related to mathematics and science teaching.

- **http://archives.math.utk.edu**—Extensive list of links to other **math- and science-related** sites.

- **http://www.ed.gov/pubs/Excelling/excelling.html**—The "Excelling in Math and Science " site sponsored by the U.S. Department of Education.

- **http://primarysource.org**—Resource center/network for K-12 teachers teaching "more inclusive" **social studies**. Five main content areas: China Studies; African-American Intellectual

History; Mayan Studies; Caribbean Studies; the American West. Useful for its links.

- **http://www.MathematicallySane.com/**—Responds to the "Math Wars." Seeks to help educators, citizens and policy-makers at all levels make a stronger case for better mathematics programs and provide a forum for reform minded mathematics educators. This site also provides a wealth of links that can support mathematics teachers with curriculum development.

- **http://www.eduplace.com/rdg/res**—Provides information and resources for K-12 balanced literacy instruction.

- **http://www.edweek.org/context/topics/issuespage .cfm?id=14**—Education Week's coverage of "Phonics and Whole Language." Offers links to related organizations and articles.

CHAPTER 6
INSTRUCTION AND
ASSESSMENT: CLASSROOMS AS
LEARNING COMMUNITIES

OVERVIEW

Chapter 6, "Instruction and Assessment: Classrooms as Learning Communities," begins with pictures of past classrooms that, as archaic as they sound, have disturbingly familiar features. As in many of today's classrooms, the teachers' job was to transmit knowledge to students in an orderly sequence of steps. However, the narrow, unidimensional design of such lessons leads most students to conclude that they're just not very smart. In contrast, cognitive and sociocultural research presses teachers to focus less on transmitting knowledge than on developing learning relationships with students. These relationships allow students to engage knowledge in ways that transform their thinking, promote their development, and over time help them realize their potential to be fully participating members of the culture. Teachers who want to change the world strive to make their classrooms places where both they and their students can be confident about everyone's ability to learn. They structure active and interactive learning activities and assessment tasks that make learning accessible to culturally and linguistically diverse groups of students.

CHAPTER HEADINGS

GENERATIVE QUESTIONS AND ACTIVITIES

Seeking a Sociocultural Pedagogy

1. One model for pursuing one's goals, a very modern one, is to break down the goal into small achievable units, accomplish one unit of the goal, and then move on to the next. But when Oakes and Lipton write about

achieving a classroom based on sociocultural learning theories and principles of social justice, they emphasize *the struggle* for such classes, rather than a surefire set of steps to achieve them. They suggest further that such a class is "an ideal—something to be pursued, but something never quite good enough to suit us." Can you think of any corresponding goals or ideals in your own life (not having to do with classroom experiences) that you expect to be a lifelong struggle, rather than an "accomplishment" that you can simply achieve and be satisfied with? Write about one such ideal and find in it parallels, if you can, to what one might face as a social-justice educator.

2. Oakes and Lipton offer a demanding set of guidelines that teachers can use "as they construct authentic and socially just classroom learning communities":
   - Teachers and students are confident that *everyone* learns well.
   - Lessons are active, multidimensional, and social.
   - Assessment enhances learning.
   - Relationships are caring and interdependent.
   - Talk and action are socially just.

If you have the opportunity to observe a classroom over time, use these guidelines to organize your observations. Otherwise, recall the details of one of your own classroom experiences and describe whether and how you experienced these elements. Note that Oakes and Lipton do not intend these guidelines to be a "Yes/No" checklist. Detail how and to what extent these dimensions are present—how and whether each guideline appears to enter into the teacher's struggle for a classroom guided by sociocultural and socially just principles.

Confidence in a Context of Difference

3. Describe a situation you experienced or observed when a public comparison undermined a student's (perhaps your own) confidence. Be sure to speculate on the *intention* of the comparison. Whom was it intended to benefit, and how? Was it intended to hurt or diminish anyone's confidence or comfort?

4. "Learned helplessness" is not a rare or exotic psychological pathology. To at least some degree it is familiar to everyone. Listen for the next adult, possibly a teacher, who says, "I'm absolutely useless when it comes to math. My wife has to balance the checkbook." Perhaps you know someone who still avoids computers. Provide one or more examples of your own learned helplessness. Is it fairly specific ("I'm not very skilled at basketball"), or is it global ("I'm a total waste at any sport that requires skill" or "I can't do anything mechanical")?

5. Think of your own experiences in which you have felt and/or observed stereotypical vulnerability of the sort described by Makeba Jones and Claude Steele (pp. 220–221). Further, even though you are dignified and polite in your public speech and expression, consider whether you might have contributed to a climate of racial vulnerability—for example, by "checking out" a racial-minority student's class performance or speech, or paying some extra attention to the home and yard upkeep of a racial-minority family in the neighborhood. Is it possible to entirely avoid making these observations? Can such observations (and thoughts?) ever be entirely invisible?

6. By exploring Claude Steele's *stereotypical vulnerability* and Daniel Solorzano's *microaggressions,* Oakes and Lipton offer a deeper look into the power and effects of race in schooling. Do these concepts help you understand how subtle expressions of stereotypes and prejudice work to disadvantage people perceived to be different? At what age do you think students can be introduced to these ideas in order to help them understand the effects of prejudice on both themselves and others?

7. Oakes and Lipton use the expression *constructing competence* to indicate an important dimension of the teacher's work. Have you ever been in a class in which the teacher practiced competent instruction but did not succeed in helping you (or others) construct your own competence? How might this teacher have modified his or her instruction to help you or others become a competent member of the classroom community? Write a detailed example.

Active, Multidimensional, and Social Instruction

8. Cognitively Guided Instruction (CGI) is an example of current research into teaching that has yet to come to the attention of many teachers, as well as many college instructors and researchers. What might be some unique challenges and special benefits to a "new" teacher who is interested in pursuing CGI further?

9. Oakes and Lipton offer brief descriptions of small-group or cooperative learning, and of scaffolding strategies and question asking. But theirs is not a book that goes extensively into teaching methods—particularly in specific school subjects. In addition to the obvious, "take a class that promises to teach those

skills," how might a prospective or experienced teacher go about acquiring the content-specific instructional skills and knowledge to become skilled at group instruction and scaffolding? What cautions might you have if you were invited to attend an afternoon "in-service" on cooperative groups or a one-day workshop on cognitively guided instruction?

10. Teaching with cooperative groups is a good example of an instructional strategy that, although always a struggle and never perfect, is usually worth the effort. Furthermore, the instructional benefits of cooperative learning are widely documented, and books, instructional materials, and training are widely available. Yet considerable resistance to cooperative learning remains, and too many teachers try out and abandon this strategy. What steps would you take if you wanted to use cooperative groups, but sensed resistance from students, parents, or teacher colleagues?

11. A classroom culture of sharing and cooperation takes effort and time to develop. Oftentimes, cooperative learning strategies are dismissed because teachers believe that whole-group instruction is a more efficient way to impart knowledge. However, effective teachers use a variety of strategies to address their students' multiple learning needs. In addition, like adults, children tend to be more productive, more alert, and less bored if they have a chance to move between activity settings rather than engaging in a single activity for a longer time. Reflect on a grade or subject you would like to teach. Think strategically about how you would plan a lesson or an instructional day. Which objectives would best be accomplished in cooperative groups? Which lessons would be most effectively taught in a whole-class format? Small-group format?

When would individual seat-work be acceptable? How might you make the learning "fun" without introducing destructive elements of competition? Give reasons for your decisions.

12. Suppose you volunteered to serve on a school's "Technology Committee," but that, other than a general interest in technology and a modest facility with a computer, you do not have extensive technology expertise. What do you think you could offer this committee as you work alongside others to learn about the available technologies and to bring them to your school?

13. In Oakes and Lipton's discussion of the "Digital Divide," they assert, "The proper role for schools must be to find the ways to prepare all students well and equally, not for schools to 'excuse' themselves by saying that some don't want to learn" (p. 243). Imagine you work in a racially, socioeconomically, and linguistically diverse high school. Develop a "Technology Access Plan" for your school. Consider that any significant school "improvement" or "reform" such as that required to shift patterns of access will have these three dimensions: (1) a **normative** dimension that addresses people's beliefs, philosophies, and attitudes regarding who can and should learn what knowledge; (2) a **political** dimension that addresses the power structures and groups that support or resist change; and (3) a **technical** dimension that addresses how organizational and teaching resources and methods are arranged for optimal learning experiences. As an alternative, find a school's current technology plan, mission, or set of objectives and analyze the degree to which the normative, political, and technical dimensions are addressed. In the likely event that

important gaps exist in this plan, fill in the gaps with your own provisions. Work with a partner or group, or make this a whole-class effort. Finally, you might consider how this very question can become the core of an engaging and highly motivational lesson for students from upper elementary to high school levels. (For an example, see www.teachingtochangetheworld.org, and look up the "Digital Divide" issue.)

14. The authors also assert that there are gender differences in access to and use of technology and that these differences are not trivial. Similar to what you did in question 13, create a plan that attempts to support gender equity in technology use and access in a large, diverse public high school.

Assessment for Learning

15. Describe an example of an assessment (look for one at as young an age as you can remember) that had a strong—even profound—effect on your schooling and/or life experiences.

16. Focus on a particular class in which you were recently enrolled. How did the type of test or the overall assessment program of that class affect your study and learning? Describe a "best example" of how an assessment helped you gain deep knowledge of a topic. Describe a "worst example" of how an assessment seemed to discourage you from deep and thorough learning.

17. Select a class with which you are familiar—one that you have recently taken or one in which you are now enrolled. List several (try five) proposals or steps you could take to make the assessment more "authentic."

For each proposal, note some likely resistance to the change: who would resist, why would they resist, and how would they explain or defend their resistance?

18. Oakes and Lipton contend that high-stakes testing has been imposed largely for political rather than educational reasons. They also draw attention to the fact that the spread of test-driven, high-stakes policies has led to an outburst of criticism that almost equals the enthusiasm of such policies' supporters. These concerns are normative (beliefs, attitudes, and philosophies), political, and technical in nature. Conduct some research about assessment measures and high-stakes testing. Write a short paper supporting your position in support of or against high-stakes testing. You may want to include the normative, political, and technical dimensions in your argument.

WEB SITES

You can link directly to all of the Web sites listed below from the *Teaching to Change the World* Web site located at www.mhhe.com/oakes2e. We recommend linking from that site, as URLs are subject to change and we will be posting updates there.

- **http://www.thirteen.org/edonline/concept2class/ month2/index_sub3.html**—Thorough exploration of "Constructivism as a Paradigm for Teaching and Learning." An interactive site that offers demonstration lessons, interviews with researchers and teachers and a good list of resources.
- **http://www.siu.edu/~deweyctr/index2.html**—The Center for Dewey Studies' home page provides

links to publications about and by John Dewey, as well as sites related to the philosophy of John Dewey.

- **http://trc.virginia.edu/tips.htm#coop**—The Teaching Resource Center at the University of Virginia offers this brief description of a few elements of cooperative learning lessons.

- **http://www.iasce.net/**—**The International Association of the Study of Cooperation in Education (IASCE)** site lists resources on cooperative learning.

- **http://www.cde.ca.gov/iasa/cooplrng.html**— California State Department of Education's **cooperative learning** Web page.

- **http://edweb.sdsu.edu/EdWeb_Folder/People/Bd odge/scaffolding.html**—"Schools, Skills, and Scaffolding on the Web." This splendid site gives a useful, concise introduction to **Vygotsky** through sophisticated Web presentation. Includes PowerPoint slides and links.

- **http://www.fairtest.org**—**The National Center for Fair and Open Testing (FairTest)** is an advocacy organization working to end the abuses, misuses, and flaws of standardized testing and ensure that evaluation of students is fair, open, and educationally sound.

- **http://www.fairtest.org/arn/High_Stakes_and_R etention_are_Class_Based_and_Racist.html** The Coalition for Educational Justice (CEJ), a grassroots, activist organization composed of teachers, students, and parents, claims that high-stakes tests are racist and unfair.

- **http://www.edletter.org/past/issues/1999- ma/human.shtml**—Harvard Educational Letter article, "The Human Cost of Over-Reliance on Tests."

- **http://scrtec.org/track/tracks/f00133.html**—Another extensive site with links upon links related to **alternative performance assessment and student portfolios.**

- **http://trc.virginia.edu/tips.htmhttp://trc.virginia.edu/tips.htm/**—Offers teaching tips on classroom assessment techniques, testing, critical thinking, cooperative learning, and more.

CHAPTER 7
CLASSROOM MANAGEMENT:
CARING AND DEMOCRATIC
COMMUNITIES

OVERVIEW

Chapter 7, "Classroom Management: Caring and Democratic Communities," offers the historical, philosophical, and research underpinnings of classroom management and student discipline practices, with an emphasis on connecting these practices with learning. It surveys the traditional legacy of management, discipline, and control on which many contemporary teachers still rely to organize classroom life. It also reviews a second tradition—caring and democratic classrooms—that, although less common, also has deep American roots. This second tradition is notably consistent with cognitive and sociocultural learning theories. The chapter concludes by calling attention to the important contributions of critical theorists who address classroom issues of power and domination and how teachers may respond to these issues as they attempt to make their classrooms socially just. This work argues that classrooms must allow children to experience democracy as well as learn about it, if they are to learn to be members of a culturally democratic community.

CHAPTER HEADINGS

GENERATIVE QUESTIONS AND ACTIVITIES

Management, Discipline, and Control: Lasting Legacies

1. Because all students have been "taught" appropriate classroom behaviors from the earliest grades (i.e., raise your hand before speaking, do not throw objects, come to class on time), many teachers believe that students should possess these "good" or "correct" learning-appropriate classroom behaviors Generate a list of reasons for classroom "misbehavior" other than this reason: that students have not learned a firm list of nonnegotiable behavioral expectations. In particular, pay attention to (or speculate on) developmental elements of sociocultural learning.

2. Consider the class in which you are now enrolled. Do you misbehave? With others, generate a list of reasons why you forego many or most of the misbehaviors that one might expect to find in K-12 classrooms. Avoid simplistic answers such as, "We're more mature." On the other hand, looking only at yourself, see if you can identify some *resistance* behaviors—actions you might take that, while not overtly defiant, preserve your autonomy while diminishing the authority or goals of the class or school.

3. What do "equitable learning communities" and conventional notions of "correct" or "good" classroom behavior have to do with one another? How do they overlap, and how are they contradictory?

4. Oakes and Lipton seem to offer a mixed view of William Glasser's "Choice Theory." While preferring Glasser's program to "overtly behaviorist classroom management programs," Oakes and Lipton criticize Glasser for neglecting "many mediating processes" within the whole school's social environment. Briefly (try for one developed paragraph), develop a list of questions you would want to ask about *any* consultant-provided or commercially available program to improve schools or teaching.

5. *__Only a Teacher.__* Oakes and Lipton refer again to early nineteenth-century schools as trying to match the organizational efficiencies of factories. These factories placed a high priority on training workers who would labor dutifully within the factories' systems. The first segment video in the *Only a Teacher* series, *A Teacher Affects Eternity,* makes a similar point, as does "Teaching in the Education Factory" from the video *Those Who Can . . . Teach.* How might students benefit from schools that follow a factory-like efficiency model? How might teachers benefit? What are possible problems for students or teachers with the model? Give examples from schools with which you are familiar.

6. What obstacles can factory-like schools present to teachers who want to make schools more humane places?

7. A central dilemma—one that continually frustrates educators and other social helpers and theorists—is to find productive ways to deliver essential help and resources to students who have not mastered the mainstream, dominant culture and language, without falling into the trap of seeing these students as "culturally deprived." Although this dilemma is unlikely ever to be fully resolved, how can sociocultural learning theory inform the discussions of teachers who want to help students preserve their unique, culturally specific, and different strengths while making sure these students can find success within the dominant culture?

8. Request printed matter, including advertising and promotional materials, from commercial (private) providers of school and/or teacher improvement programs that offer learning and discipline goals (such as Glasser's Choice Theory, Assertive Discipline, Sylvan Learning Centers, Avid, and others) to schools. Include among your requests programs that are "nonprofit," associated with public universities, or have other relationships with public or noncommercial entities (e.g., Success for All, Cognitively Guided Instruction), since these programs also "compete" to have schools buy their services or materials. Develop a list of criteria for evaluating how useful these programs might be in accomplishing what they promise to accomplish. In particular, assess the promotional materials for their attention to or neglect of sociocultural principles.

9. Consider Nel Noddings' view of *care* as a "continuous search for competence." How might this view both encompass and extend your previous view of what it means to care? Think about how the search for competence in others enters into relationships with one's children, parents, friends, colleagues, teachers, and students, and how those relationships might change if greater attention were paid to the search for competence. Consider also, how competence is *constructed* and *co*-constructed within these relationships. Describe an example of the co-construction of competence in a relationship that you have experienced or observed. Keep in mind that while searching for competence may result in a profound, deeply memorable, and life-changing understanding, it may also proceed in cumulative micro-steps.

10. Oakes and Lipton have previously criticized "Assertive Discipline" and other rule-oriented programs designed to control student behavior. In this chapter they strengthen their criticism with the work of Noddings, Fogel, Howes and Richie, Noblitt, and other psychologists, researchers, and theorists. But do Oakes and Lipton and other progressives offer a compelling alternative to behavioral methods? What would you say to a critic who would claim that Noblitt's "dogged determination" really means "put up with misbehavior while the kids run all over you"? In other words, will an emphasis on care lead adults to abandon their responsibility to teach the young how to behave?

11. Oakes and Lipton cite some questions that Alfie Kohn proposes can help "turn classrooms into places where discipline problems rarely happen." ("What makes

school awful sometimes?" "What can we do this year to make sure things go better?" "Suppose you hurt someone's feelings, or did something even worse. How would you want us, the rest of the community, to help you then?" and "What if someone else acted that way? How could we help that person?") How can teachers and students construct a safe and caring learning community? Answer/discuss these questions with a group in your own class. Propose a few additional questions that are specifically tailored to your class context and discuss those.

Socially Just Classrooms: Doing Democracy

12. How does this or another class provide and/or fail to provide culturally relevant opportunities for your learning? In what respects do the professor and/or classmates understand or not understand you well enough to respond to you in culturally relevant ways?

13. If you are largely comfortable with the cultural environment of your current class(es), imagine yourself in a classroom in which your culture was very poorly understood and you felt unconnected to the content or people. In that case, what about you and your background would it be important for others to understand and accept so that you could feel comfortable, included, and trusting in that environment?

Creating Classroom Communities Is a Struggle

14. Create list of considerations that would go into a year-long management plan for the grade you teach or would like to teach. Be sure to include details such as seating plans, everyday procedures (pencil sharpening,

attendance, going to the bathroom, going to lunch, changing classes, etc.), the development of classroom rules or community agreements, office referrals, and home contacts. Working with a group, you should be able to come up with a very long list. Next, identify for each of these considerations (when possible) one "Potential for Good" and one "Potential for Harm." What theory supports your assessment of these potentials for good or harm?

[1] Alfie Kohn, Beyond Discipline: From Compliance to Community (Alexandria, VA: Association for Supervision and Curriculum Development, 1996), pp. 114–115.

WEB SITES

You can link directly to all of the Web sites listed below from the *Teaching to Change the World* Web site located at www.mhhe.com/oakes2e. We recommend linking from that site, as URLs are subject to change and we will be posting updates there.

- **http://www.nwrel.org/comm/topics/classman.html/**—A collection of resources focusing on **Classroom Management**, sponsored by the North Western Regional Educational Laboratory.

- **http://jaring.nmhu.edu/classman.htm**—A page of links related to **classroom management**.

- **http://www.wglasser.com/**—The **William Glasser** Institute. Features an explanation of choice theory, a biography, and much more.

- **http://www.infed.org/thinkers/et-pest.htm**—This well-written site about **Johann Pestalozzi** includes graphic, biography, bibliography, and links.

- **http://www.infed.org/thinkers/et-froeb.htm**—A brief introduction to **Friedrich Froebel**. The Infed site—for informal education—offers interesting links to perspectives on educational principles in contexts outside of schools.

- **http://www.geocities.com/Athens/Forum/7905/weblinks.html**—Many links to **Froebel** sites.

- **http://www.ed.uiuc.edu/PES/92_docs/Noddings.htm**—"Excellence as a Guide to Educational Conversation." Read this engaging and persuasive essay by **Nel Noddings**.

- **http://www.ascd.org/readingroom/edlead/9509/kohn.html**—An interview: "Punished By Rewards? A Conversation with **Alfie Kohn**."

- http://www.splcenter.org/teachingtolerance.html
  —The official site of **Teaching Tolerance** National
  education project "dedicated to helping teachers
  foster equity, respect and understanding in the
  classroom and beyond." Magazine and videos.
  Classroom resources and activities. Reading list.

- http://www.usdoj.gov/kidspage—The **U.S.
  Department of Justice** Web site includes a page
  called "Hateful Acts Hurt Kids," which includes
  classroom ideas that promote discussion among
  children, parents, and teachers about prejudice,
  discrimination, and related issues.

- http://www.rethinkingschools.org—**Rethinking
  Schools** provides resources and networks for
  teachers seeking practices that match social-justice
  values.

- http://www.nccj.org—Home page of the **National
  Conference for Community and Justice**, a human
  relations organization dedicated to fighting bias,
  bigotry, and racism in America.

- http://www.tribes.com/index.html—Home page
  of **Tribes**, featuring practical strategies to develop
  cooperative and safe classroom communities

THE *ONLY A TEACHER* VIDEO SERIES

Relevant Video Segments:

A Teacher Affects Eternity **(Video 1)**
"A Teacher Affects Eternity" (5:00–19:15)

Those Who Can Teach **(Video 2)**
"Teaching in the Education Factory" (32:06–45:20)

CHAPTER 8
GROUPING AND CATEGORICAL PROGRAMS: CAN SCHOOLS TEACH *ALL* CHILDREN WELL?

OVERVIEW

Chapter 8, "Grouping and Categorical Programs: Can Schools Teach *All* Children Well?," deals with the often-controversial ways in which schools respond to differences in students' abilities, achievements, and behaviors. Schools commonly categorize and separate children into groups that appear to be similar—or homogeneous—in order to address their needs. Many times, these practices limit rather than expand students' learning opportunities, and children of color and those from low-income families disproportionately feel these negative effects. The chapter surveys the history and social theory that link race, class, and culture to these seemingly objective and technical practices of schooling. It also explores how educators attempt to give students the attention and resources they need without isolating and alienating them from the mainstream.

CHAPTER HEADINGS

GENERATIVE QUESTIONS AND ACTIVITIES

Making Distinctions

1. Once again, Oakes and Lipton set a current schooling practice in its historical context—in this chapter, grouping students. Many widely used survey-of-education books place far less emphasis on connecting particular school practices, such as curriculum decision-making, classroom management, or grouping, with their historical antecedents—particularly those antecedents that have political and social bearing. Is this historical context necessary? Interesting, but not essential? A distraction from the real issues of how schools today operate? Of course, the authors would defend their practice. Would you? To support your arguments, review copies of other textbooks that are commonly used for courses similar to the one in which you are now reading *Teaching to Change the World*. Compare the books' treatments of several topics—including grouping.

2. Review your own personal history of grouping identification—that which you experienced and/or that which you observed. Describe the satisfaction and/or disappointments you felt. Did you, your parents, or anyone at school ever question or challenge the label or identification? Did you have friends or siblings who had a different label? Did "your" group represent a racial or ethnic cross section of the school, or did you notice some groups had overrepresentations or

87

underrepresentations by race, gender, or ethnicity? How did you make sense of all this at the time, and what do you think now?

3. Some schools make an aggressive effort to recruit students of color into their "top" tracks such as honors, gifted, or AP classes. What can be some unintended consequences of such policies?

4. Observe a "special education" class and interview the teachers or talk with a parent of a child in a "special education" program. Ask what characteristics set "special education" children apart from other children. How do schools discover which children are "special"? How does this educator or parent describe the "special education" as different from what other children receive? How does the school decide what each "special" child needs? How do they judge whether their "special" efforts are successful? To what standards are these programs held accountable?

5. Observe a "gifted" class and interview the teachers or talk with a parent of a child in a "gifted" program. Ask what characteristics set "gifted" children apart from other children. How do schools discover which children are "gifted"? How does this educator or parent describe the "gifted education" as different from what other children receive? How does the school decide what each "gifted" child needs? How do they judge whether their "gifted" efforts are successful? To what standards are these programs held accountable?

Dilemmas with Homogeneous Grouping

6. Oakes and Lipton argue not only that grouping categories themselves are not accurate or fair ways of

organizing students for instruction, but that the actual assignment of students to those categories is deeply flawed. They identify several factors that make students' placements inaccurate, subjective, and open to manipulation: arbitrarily designed and enforced placement criteria and procedures; the fallibility of testing; parents' and students' own activism; and structural constraints such as limited resources and scheduling problems. Select a school and determine whether and how exceptions to these grouping practices are made. First, ask for public documents (course descriptions, grouping policies, waiver policies, etc.) that have bearing on grouping practices; then interview school personnel regarding exceptions to placement criteria, paying particular attention to patterns of exceptions according to race, gender, language, or economic status.

7. Many advocates of ability grouping and gifted programs in academic subjects argue that these practices make sense in the same way that selecting the "best" athletes for competitive sports teams and the "best" musicians for the concert band makes sense. What similarities and differences do you see in these practices? Does the argument make sense to you? Would you argue the same way if you knew you were a "gifted" student as you would if you knew that you were a "slow" student?

Accommodating Diversity Without Sorting
Implementing Heterogeneous Grouping

8. Seek out examples of schools or school districts that are attempting to reduce, modify, or eliminate tracking. Identify and describe the changes in structure or procedures, the successes, and the difficulties. Look for

provisions that attempt to preserve some of the "privileges" of high-track placement. Look especially for evidence on whether detracking has prompted the teachers or schools to base their instruction more strongly on sociocultural learning perspectives.

9. ***Only a Teacher.*** The third video in the series, *Educating to End Inequity,* portrays the history of race-based segregation in American public schools as well as addresses the way in which segregation plays out in schools today. How are segregation and tracking related? In what ways are detracking efforts and desegregation measures as well as the responses to them also alike? Different?

WEB SITES

You can link directly to all of the Web sites listed below from the *Teaching to Change the World* Web site located at www.mhhe.com/oakes2e. We recommend linking from that site, as URLs are subject to change and we will be posting updates there.

- **http://ncrve.berkeley.edu/AllInOne/MDS-746.html**—National Center for Research in Vocational Education at the University of California at Berkeley developed a **resource guide concerning inclusion, detracking**, ability grouping, mainstreaming, and cooperative learning.
- **http://www.edweek.org/context/topics/issuespage .cfm?id=47** *Education Week*'s background and past stories on **special education and inclusion**.
- **http://www.gifted.uconn.edu/nrcgt.html**—Home page for The National Research Center on the **Gifted and Talented**.

90

- **http://www.edb.utexas.edu/coe/depts/ci/bilingue/resources.html**—Bilingual education resources on the Internet.

- **http://www.ncbe.gwu.edu/miscpubs/ncrcdsll**—The National Center for Research on Cultural Diversity and Second Language Learning. Includes links to articles that draw connections between language minority education and sociocultural learning theory.

- **http://www.edweek.org/context/topics/issuespage.cfm?id=26** Education Week's past articles and links related to **tracking**.

- **http://www.ncbe.gwu.edu/**—The National Clearinghouse for English Language Acquisition (formerly the National Clearinghouse for Bilingual Education, but was changed because of the "No Child Left Behind Act" of 2001).

- **http://www.bilingualeducation.org/resources.htm**—California Association of Bilingual Educators' (CABE) list of resources for those interested in bilingual education, the education of immigrant students, language acquisition, and teaching for social justice.

THE *ONLY A TEACHER* VIDEO SERIES

Relevant Video Segments:

Educating to End Inequity (Video 3)
"Educating to End Inequity" (5:47)

CHAPTER 9
THE SCHOOL CULTURE: WHERE GOOD TEACHING MAKES SENSE

OVERVIEW

Chapter 9, "The School Culture: Where Good Teaching Makes Sense," identifies theory- and research-based characteristics of schools that support excellent and democratic learning and teaching. These characteristics include opportunities to learn, an environment that makes learning seem inevitable, structures that allow teachers to know their students and their community well, and conditions that allow teachers to care and work hard. These cultural elements are necessary for teachers to be able to challenge all their students to do rigorous, intellectually demanding work. The chapter describes several current, progressive reform projects based around *inquiry*—a mode of conversation that elicits from all members of the school community their understanding of the school's environment for rigorous and socially just learning. These inquiry-based school reforms help individuals clarify others' and their own perceptions and help translate shared beliefs and values into democratic action. Finally, the chapter explores how schools can help parents become engaged in supporting actions that benefit all the students at the school.

CHAPTER HEADINGS

GENERATIVE QUESTIONS AND ACTIVITIES

Schools as Cultures

1. Oakes and Lipton note that when one is immersed in a culture, he or she may hardly be aware of the culture's characteristics or effects. Because the culture represents what is "normal," most K-12 students (as well as most adults) pay little conscious attention to how the culture affects them. In fact, the cultural value for independence, for "being my own person," and for rejecting peer pressure is so strong that young students and teenagers will often deny that the culture has any effect on them at all—proclaiming themselves immune from fads, school values, or other cultural influences. Reflect on your own experiences within your school cultures—paying particular attention to those times when you felt somehow at odds with the school's academic press. Perhaps your disposition was to work harder or be more focused on school achievement than what the school seemed to support. Perhaps you were inclined to work less hard, but were "carried along" by the press for high achievement in a class or at the school—it seemed as if everyone worked hard and valued academic achievement, so you might as well, also.

2. It is not uncommon for a school to have a different presses for different students—perhaps according to academic "ability" track. Comment on whether an institutional press for high achievement was applied similarly to all students at your high school—in particular, on whether the press for high achievement extended to all students across racial, gender, and economic lines.

3. Some classes seem to spend a lot of time in activities that have little to do with learning valued knowledge (*any* valued knowledge—not just that related to the subject being taught). Often, students and teacher seem to "cooperate" in keeping the class occupied with nonacademic, time-killing activities. With a group of colleagues, write and perform a 5-minute skit that incorporates as many as possible of the "typical" strategies you have seen students and teachers employ for *not* using time productively.

4. Keep a record of specific adult behaviors at a school (including exact quotes and campus activities) that show how high or low the school's press for academic achievement is. Pay particular attention to contradictory "messages" or behaviors that on the surface seem to be pressing for or against achievement but upon closer examination may say the opposite.

5. Not all teachers who have credentials and are experts in the subject they teach are very good teachers. Yet some teachers who have a weak background can be highly motivating—especially if they are fascinated by the course topics and position themselves as eager learners alongside the students. Write a profile of such teachers based on your personal experience and/or observation. Add your thoughts as to how these teachers' behaviors are in part influenced by the school culture.

6. Oakes and Lipton observe that teachers are commonly "tracked." That is, teachers with less status, less training, or lower reputations are assigned to teach students who perform, generally, less well, whereas highly qualified teachers with strong reputations are more likely to teach students in higher-level classes. Describe your observations of and/or experience with

this phenomenon. Is this a practice that is openly discussed at schools with which you are familiar? What do you suppose (or what have you heard) are the most common reasons given for teacher tracking? Respond to these reasons with arguments for randomly assigning teachers or for making sure that all students have equal access to the most qualified teachers.

7. With a particular school in mind, compile a list of ten policy, curriculum, resource, or other changes that you believe would improve the school culture and markedly improve students' achievement. Explain how these changes are directly or indirectly aligned with making the school attuned to sociocultural learning principles, and how they are more sensitive to social-justice concerns. Where you can distinguish between them, include both a particular practice and the more general rule or policy.

8. Oakes and Lipton assert that in order for college to be genuinely accessible, students must see their cultural identities as integral to college preparation and attendance rather than as something they must overcome. Given that, what could you do as a teacher to promote college access for culturally and linguistically diverse students? Using the grade you would like to teach as a starting point, design an age-appropriate lesson or set of lessons you think would promote college-going identities among your students. Alternatively, consider that developing a college-going identity takes place over many years with students who experience countless encouraging acts. Brainstorm a list of activities or classroom routines that could, over time, help students believe that college is for people who look like and speak like them.

9. *Only a Teacher. Educating to End Inequity*, the third video in the *Only a Teacher* video series, portrays American public schools as institutions that historically have sought to assimilate non-white and immigrant students into "American culture." According to the video, schools have attempted to eradicate "other" cultures and languages through the curriculum and through the overall institutional culture. The video also portrays Urban Academy, an alternative high school in New York City that attempts to reverse this historical role. How do the curriculum, management, and overall structure and culture of Urban Academy differ from those of more traditional schools? As an additional "thought experiment," imagine that you were trying to convince administrators of an early Indian boarding school to adopt features of Urban Academy. State several of your proposals and follow them with what you would expect to hear as arguments against making the changes.

Access to Care

10. List several ways in which you have seen teachers show they care about and for their students. List several ways in which an entire school culture can show care. In each case, contrast these ways of caring with alternative ways—ways teachers or schools sometimes act—that show less care.

11. In the September 25, 2001, issue of the *Christian Science Monitor*, third-year teacher Mary Hendra writes about her discussions with students following the events of September 11. The authors, taking their lead from Alfie Kohn, argue that these types of discussions

allow schools and teachers to be wiser and more humane—that they "help children locate themselves in widening circles of care that extend beyond the self, beyond country, to all humanity" (p. 378). Still, teachers who address sensitive issues such as September 11 may be criticized by parents or administrators; they may also encounter resistance among their students. What might teachers do to "set up" this type of frank and difficult discussion—not only to lessen risk to themselves, but to be sure that the discussion or activity they have in mind is, in fact, responsible and sensitive?

Inquiry and Activism

12. A common criticism of team teaching is that it may turn out that one teacher teaches twice as many students while the other teacher simply has some "free time." Then they trade. However, Oakes and Lipton point out that team teaching is at the heart of many teaching reforms. List the benefits of team teaching that you can think of or have observed. How are these benefits consistent with sociocultural perspectives of teaching?

WEB SITES

You can link directly to all of the Web sites listed below from the *Teaching to Change the World* Web site located at www.mhhe.com/oakes2e. We recommend linking from that site, as URLs are subject to change and we will be posting updates there.

- **http://www.essentialschools.org**—The official U.S. site of the **Coalition of Essential Schools**. Includes information beyond the ten principles.

- **http://www.acceleratedschools.net**—Henry Levin's **Accelerated Schools Project**'s home page. Includes a project description, history, accomplishments of participating schools, and a research base.

- **http://www.rethinkingschools.org/Archives/15_02/Subt152.htm** A *Rethinking Schools* article addressing "What happens when schools disrespect students' cultural heritage and when teachers fail to listen to students." Includes excerpts from **Angela Valenzuela's** book *Subtractive Schooling.*

- **http://www.ruralchallengepolicy.org/esymposium/keynote-meier.html**-A keynote address by educator **Deborah Meier**, entitled "Our Challenge: To Set the Highest Possible National Standard—for Human Relationships."

THE *ONLY A TEACHER* VIDEO SERIES

Relevant Video Segments:

***Educating to End Inequity* (Video 3)**
"Educating to End Inequity" (5:47)

CHAPTER 10
CONNECTIONS WITH FAMILIES
AND COMMUNITIES

OVERVIEW

Chapter 10, "Connections with Families and Communities," explores the roles that parents and communities play in schooling. The chapter addresses a number of parent and community involvement strategies while calling into question the notions that all parental involvement is beneficial and that little parental involvement necessarily signals a lack of educational interest. In addition, consistent with other chapters in the book, the discussion of parental involvement is situated in a sociocultural context that also considers schools as institutions that have the power to promote or impede social justice. Finally, the chapter's focus on the experiences of students and parents of color presses us to creatively reconceptualize traditional notions of parent and community involvement.

CHAPTER HEADINGS

GENERATIVE QUESTIONS AND ACTIVITIES

Laments about Parent and Community Involvement:

Too Little or Too Much

1. Oakes and Lipton explain that school failure is often attributed to cultural or genetic deficits in the students, or to a deficit of proper parenting or commitment to education. Think about a school

with which you are familiar. Describe an example of a school program that might reflect these "deficit" attitudes about students, families, or communities. How might you modify the program to counter deficit attitudes? Why would your new program be more effective?

2. Although schools may perpetuate deficit thinking about students they serve, deficit attitudes generally emerge and are reinforced outside of schools. Where in society do you receive messages that foster the idea that immigrant communities, poor parents, and parents of color do not value education? What are the roots of these attitudes? Why do you think these messages often go unquestioned?

3. Many studies have reported on parents' attitudes toward schooling. Consistently, education is a top priority for the families surveyed, including poor families and people with culturally and linguistically diverse backgrounds. Considering these strong values, do schools do enough to give students from these families preparation for higher education that is comparable to wealthier white students' preparation? Give an actual case if you have observed, read about, or experienced one.

4. Imagine you are a teacher in a school that serves culturally and linguistically diverse students. At this school, many of the teachers maintain deficit views about the students and their parents. As a new teacher, how might you begin to challenge these views? How can you be effective while building trusting long-term relationships with parents, students, and colleagues who might have very

different views? Describe an actual or hypothetical interaction in which you help a parent or colleague take on a different understanding of parent involvement.

5. Brainstorm ways in which your school can support low-income parents, parents of color, and non-English-speaking parents in feeling more comfortable at your school site. What resources would you need to make this a reality?

6. Oakes and Lipton argue that in schools that serve diverse students, white, affluent parents often pressure schools in ways that undermine high-quality learning opportunities for students of color, students whose families are poor, and students who have not been designated as destined for high achievement. Describe a situation in which affluent parents have exercised their power and privilege to manipulate the system in order to "protect" their own children. Brainstorm ideas on how the school can institutionally respond to these types of demands in order to provide equitable learning opportunities for all students.

7. Oakes and Lipton describe a situation in which parents used their own status and expertise (as scientists and mathematicians) to condemn an academic program for failing to prepare their children for the rigors of the university. It can be argued that this type of involvement undermines teachers' professionalism. In arguing for more community empowerment, do we also open the door for this type of "overbearing" parental involvement? Choose one side of this double-edged argument. Stage a debate in which each side must

substantiate its position regarding appropriate limits or levels of parental involvement. Over a period of weeks or months, watch local newspapers for evidence of this type of dilemma.

8. One cannot imagine any significant American constituency being *against* parent involvement. Yet people in schools are clearly ambivalent about how to find proper roles for all parents. Further, even in schools that profess a desire for parent involvement there may be counter-efforts and attitudes that work against meaningful involvement. Begin a list of what schools do in the name of parent involvement. Then critique the many ways in which the schools might undermine or diminish the effectiveness of these involvement activities. Generally, you might ask whether the school seems more concerned with *pleasing* parents than they are with *involving* them. For example, you might list "open house" as a way schools involve parents. Your critique might suggest that an open house might not "involve" parents if parents do nothing more than listen to teachers talk for a few minutes about the curriculum.

9. On page 400, a first-year teacher describes a situation in which a white parent asks the teacher to move her child's seat to prevent her from sitting next to a Spanish-speaking child. In your struggle to be a socially just teacher, how would you respond to a parent who approached you with a concern that reflects racist beliefs? With people in your class or group, set up a role-playing demonstration in which one person acts the part of the teacher, and another takes on the role of the parent. Do this only in an environment where there is great trust, experienced

"observers," and ample opportunity to debrief when the role-play is over.

10. It can be argued that one of the reasons affluent parents exercise their power in harmful ways is that there are limited spaces in competitive courses and higher education. Because we cannot count on additional spots opening up at the university level, what are some suggestions for providing students with more equitable educational opportunities?

11. Clearly the authors believe that no one group should dominate the school's attention when it comes to providing a fair education to all students. Do you agree with this position? Or do you believe that in a democratic environment the parents with the skills and gumption to make themselves heard are bound to wind up with greater influence? Perhaps you believe that both statements are partly true. Where do you stand on this issue, and what might schools do if they were to act more in accordance with your beliefs?

Forging Helpful Connections

12. Joyce Epstein and Mavis Sanders argue that schools, families, and communities must build partnerships in order to promote learning and success among students. What do you think "partnership" means? Do you think schools currently want to be equal partners with parents? If schools, families, and communities do forge authentic partnerships, what might the positive outcomes be? The negative outcomes?

13. Oakes and Lipton posit that Epstein's typology presumes that school is a neutral place and that it is the job of the families to develop practices that match those of the school so that their children can succeed. How does Epstein's typology reflect the assumption that schools are politically neutral spaces? Provide some examples of this phenomenon from a school with which you are familiar.

14. The authors describe many of the current practices that involve parents as too focused on individual students or school-defined categories of students. They suggest considering instead what will be good for the whole school or community. What would this look like? Construct two cases (for example, a school's decision to provide "enrichment" or "catch-up" activities for a particular group) that address the same issue—one case from an individualistic perspective and one from a collective or structural perspective.

15. In the early 1900s, reformers in a number of cities advocated making the public schools "social centers" to provide social and educational services to the broader community of poor, often oppressed urban dwellers. Many of the ideas about the social ills that characterized urban centers during that time period are depicted in the1955 film *The Blackboard Jungle*. (See reference below.) Show a clip of this film to students. Is there a modern film that addresses current issues in a similar fashion? How are the issues the same? Different? How are proposed remedies from the early twentieth century (making schools "social centers") to address issues that cross the school threshold into the social issues of home and community? How was the social-

center perspective preserved in mid-twentieth-century schools, and what is comparable today?

16. James Comer's model provides many necessary services and resources to community members, but some might argue that it is based on deficit assumptions. Would that make the remedies necessarily flawed? What questions would you ask to help you determine whether Comer's model escapes deficit approaches? What modifications to the program might you suggest?

Bridging the Cultures of Schools and Families

17. Oakes and Lipton advocate a "bridge-building" model as opposed to a "service-providing" model (in which service and empowerment flow from helpers to clients). Show segments of the film *Women of Summer* about Bryn Mawr's Depression-era summer school for working women. (See reference below.) How does this documentary provide examples of the bridge-building model? The service-providing model?

18. Discuss Luis Moll's notion of the "Funds of Knowledge." Draw comparisons between Addams' 1900-era ideas about visiting the homes and workplaces of community members and Moll's ideas about teachers conducting home visits.

19. Read the introduction of Angel Valenzuela's *Subtractive Schooling,* where she attributes the academic failure of Mexican-American students to their feelings of not being cared for at school (see reference below). W. E. B. DuBois' statement that a proper education includes a *sympathetic touch*

champions a similar point. Think about schools you have experienced. Did you feel cared for? Actually, consider whether the *teacher* felt cared for. What aspects of the school made this happen (if it did)? Do you think this affected student learning? Be as specific as you can.

20. Mary Ann Pacheco provides a great example that emphasizes the need to reinforce families' cultural beliefs while helping their children succeed. She does this by discussing with parents her own experiences in higher education. Brainstorm additional characteristics that are valued in higher education but may reflect white, middle-class preferences that place culturally diverse students at a disadvantage. What are some strategies for addressing these issues with low-income parents of color in the way that Mary Ann suggests—that is, reinforcing their own values and beliefs simultaneously?

21. Zeba Palomino discusses her success at getting parents to attend Back to School Night by personally calling to invite them and being able to communicate with them in Spanish. What are some strategies that you might use to make parents feel comfortable in your classroom if you do not speak their language? Suggest some ways to involve parents more profoundly—that is, taking it further than merely inviting them to your classroom.

22. Benjamin Chang refers to a curriculum that reflects parent and community values. Design a lesson plan and/or thematic unit that incorporates parent knowledge and expertise without imposing the

white, middle-class expectations/values that
Benjamin describes.

23. Oakes and Lipton along with Vivienne Paley
    suggest that community-based curriculum often
    requires that teachers learn about and confront the
    racism and discrimination that many families
    experience in communities and schools. In turn, this
    requires that teachers reflect deeply about their own
    positionalities (racial and class status) in relation to
    the children they serve. Given that this can be an
    extraordinarily difficult and sensitive task, how
    might schools support teachers in this type of work?

24. Currently, there are principals who separate parents
    into ethnic or racial groups to discuss issues such as
    standardized test scores. Some have argued such
    practices are patronizing and racist. Miriam Rogers,
    an African American parent, however, believes that
    WRAAP, an African American parent group, is
    necessary and powerful. Although one-race
    groupings can easily generate concerns and
    suspicions, describe some circumstances in which
    such groupings might produce benefits.

Partnering with Families and Communities in Educational Activism

25. The authors argue for a radically different approach
    to linking poor parents with schools. They propose
    to engage low-income families and community
    members in critically examining their children's
    schooling opportunities and in taking action that
    promotes change. However, this creates unique
    difficulties both for teachers of color and for white
    teachers. What challenges might be shared by both

groups of teachers? What particular challenges might be faced by white teachers? By teachers of color?

26. Who, at a school with which you are familiar, is most responsible for involving parents? Interview this person (consider an e-mail exchange if you know of someone out of town) to determine how this person views his or her responsibilities.

27. Why do you think the PTA and many other parent organizations seek to "improve" schools as they are rather than challenging schools to undertake reforms that are consistent with social justice? A dilemma for social-justice teachers is whether to try to work within these powerful organizations or to place their energies in participating and organizing groups without an official connection with the schools. Can and should teachers try to affect the goals of these parent organizations?

28. Attend one or more evening meetings of a parent or community group that deals with community issues. If school representatives or people with a special interest in the community's schools are present, what roles do they play? Does the group seem to be working *with* the schools to greatest advantage? What are members doing to accomplish this work, and what might they do differently? Is the group well informed about conditions and problems at schools—including political, cultural, resource, and academic conditions?

29. Multicultural education finds its roots in the Civil Rights Movement, Afro-centric schools, and social activism. Examine a multicultural lesson or unit (or

design your own) that incorporates social action while emphasizing academic rigor. What opportunities are there to ensure that the learning is embedded in social action and reflects the needs of the community? How will you balance state-mandated standards and content frameworks with community input?

30. Describe a project for engaging parents at a school you attended or where you work(ed). Were the three elements of the Ganz model (relationship, common understanding, and action) employed? If so, how? If not, how could the project be modified to include these components?

31. Oakes and Lipton argue that an important part of reaching out to parents is emphasizing the idea that parents should focus their efforts on gaining an excellent education for *all* children rather than just their own. What can teachers do to promote this attitude among parents? Among other teachers?

32. Describe various forms of parental involvement that you feel reflect sociocultural notions of schooling. Which practices do not? Explain.

WEB SITES

You can link directly to all of the Web sites listed below from the *Teaching to Change the World* Web site located at www.mhhe.com/oakes2e. We recommend linking from that site, as URLs are subject to change and we will be posting updates there.

- http://www.ncpie.org—The **National Coalition for Parent Involvement in Education** home page. Provides links to numerous family–education organizations, family–community organizations, government agencies, higher education and research organizations, and state parent information resource centers.

- **http://tcla.gseis.ucla.edu/democracy/community/lynwood.html** An article looking at the **mobilization of parents in the urban community** of Lynwood, California, from *Teaching to Change LA,* the **online journal** of IDEA, **UCLA's Institute for Democracy, Education and Access.**

- **http://tcla.gseis.ucla.edu/divide/community/lynwood.html Lynwood Parents Investigate Technology Resources in Their Community.** An additional *Teaching to Change LA* article, written by Laila Hasan, director of the **UCLA Parent Project.**

http://www.gse.harvard.edu/~hfrp/projects/fine/announcements/01may.html- Harvard University's Family Research Project home page.

- **http://www.csos.jhu.edu/p2000/default.htm—** Johns Hopkins University's **National Network of Partnership Schools** site explores ways of developing productive programs of school–family–community partnerships.

- **http://www.gse.harvard.edu/~hfrp/projects/fine/resources/bibliography/work-family.html-** A selected bibliography of resources that look at family involvement and civic engagement among working families.

VIDEO AND BOOK REFERENCES

Bauman, S. & Heller, R. (Producers and Directors) (1986). *The Women of Summer: The Bryn Mawr Summer School for Women Workers, 1921–1938.* New York: Women of Summer, Inc.; Filmakers Library [distributor], 1985. One videocassette (55 min.): sd., col. with b&w sequences. *(A history of the Bryn Mawr Summer School for Women Workers (1921–1938) as seen through the eyes of its alumnae and other participants fifty years later, using unearthed diaries, letters, and historical film footage along with oral histories.)*

Brooks, R. (Writer and Director), and Berman, P.S. (Producer). (1955/ 1996). *Blackboard Jungle* [Motion Picture]. Los Angeles: MGM Vintage Classics/ Warner Home Video. (1 hour 30 minutes.)

Valenzuela, A. (1999) *Subtractive Schooling: U.S.-Mexican Youth and the Politics of Caring.* Albany: State University of New York Press.

CHAPTER 11
TEACHING TO CHANGE THE WORLD: A PROFESSION AND A HOPEFUL STRUGGLE

OVERVIEW

Chapter 11, "Teaching to Change the World: A Profession and a Hopeful Struggle," draws parallels among teachers' work in American schools, John Dewey's progressivism, Paulo Freire's pedagogy of hope, the nation's social movements for civil and human rights, and Cornel West's prophetic pragmatism. The authors assert that *hopeful struggle* best describes how teachers can work to change their teaching, their schools, and the world. The chapter grounds this struggle for high-quality and socially just schooling in current thinking about the future of democratic institutions in our postmodern world, and in the experiences of teachers engaged in that struggle.

CHAPTER HEADINGS

GENERATIVE QUESTIONS AND ACTIVITIES

Teaching to Change the World: *A Profession and a Hopeful Struggle*

1. Oakes and Lipton refer to teachers who enter the teaching profession because of their commitment to teach for social justice. What do you think they mean by social justice? Would you offer an alternative definition, or do you largely accept Oakes and Lipton's definition? Do you consider yourself to be a social-justice teacher? Why or why not?

2. Oakes and Lipton observe that "teaching for social justice—teaching to change the world—is less often the object of discussion in many teacher education programs, less often shared in school faculty rooms, less often proposed in newspaper editorials than the other reasons for becoming a teacher." Are these observations and views consistent with your own experience and observations? Explain your agreement or disagreement.

3. Clearly, the authors would link social justice inseparably to the public discussion of *any* educational issue. What are some of the stronger or more surprising links between social justice and education you have learned about in this book? Are any of the links between social justice and education incomplete?

4. Many theories can be used to support social-justice teaching. At this point in your experience, what theories (or parts of theories) seem most intriguing, most promising to you for helping you to make sense out of schools and your own teaching? Give an example of when theory (for example, sociocultural theory, critical pedagogy, or cognitive learning theory) has helped guide your understanding of what you observe or experience in a classroom.

Resisting the Pressure to Conform or to Leave

5. The authors point to a long list of challenges faced by teachers who work in poor urban and rural schools. However, in the spirit of educators such as Freire and Dewey, they also suggest that teachers who stay in the profession do so because they think of democracy as an ongoing struggle—a struggle in which they are eager to participate. On the other hand, many people entering the profession are looking for something else. They would like to "settle in" to a well-equipped school with well-trained colleagues and where nearly all the students come well prepared to learn the teachers' lessons. There, the most significant challenges are in refining one's own personal skills and competencies with a few obstacles set up by factors beyond the teacher's control. Compare this commonly held desire with the democratic and social-justice challenges above. What do you look forward to? What worries you?

6. First-year teacher Dawne Yusi discusses balancing her commitment to fight injustice with her simultaneous need to protect herself emotionally from some of the painful issues she confronts in the

community where she teaches. A similar tension exists when teachers and students want to address social issues that can be so overwhelming that both teacher and students risk losing the hopeful feelings with which they began. Given this tension, brainstorm some age-appropriate guidelines for addressing "social-justice" concerns for the grade level you (hope to) teach. How do you imagine achieving this balance?

7. Oakes and Lipton emphasize an ongoing process rather than a particular end goal in the struggle for social justice (to struggle *for* social justice is to engage in social justice). Out of this struggle, they are hopeful that tangible social-justice changes will take place. Others find this too timid an approach. They argue that until educators and others directly confront the economic, political, and social inequalities that are at the root of injustice, little can be gained toward making schools more socially just. Which of these positions do you identify with more strongly? Is it possible to subscribe to some of both? Describe where you stand.

8. Freire emphasizes the role that hope plays in the struggle for social justice, yet asserts, "the idea that hope alone will transform the world . . . is an excellent route to hopelessness, pessimism, and fatalism" (p. 436). How do you make sense of this paradoxical position? What does Freire mean? Give some practical examples.

9. The authors and first-year teachers Michelle Calva and Sarine Gureghian maintain that in order to remain focused on students' most essential needs while simultaneously coping with working conditions that emphasize efficiency, teachers must have a solid theoretical grounding as well as a clear philosophy of education. Think about your own personal philosophy of education. What are the theories and theorists that inspire and guide you? Why?

10. Oakes and Lipton assert, "No matter how modest the beginnings, there are opportunities waiting for teachers to participate in building a social-justice community that helps to shape their work lives and their personal and professional goals" (p. 440). This statement reflects the authors' belief that urban teachers who combine their commitments to student learning and social justice are more fulfilled and are therefore less likely to leave the teaching profession. Oftentimes, this commitment to social justice is manifested through the teacher's own activism and by the alliances she or he forges with members of the community. Consider the school where you work now. How well do you know that community? What resources are available to the families that live and work there? How can the relationships you develop with allies in the community also translate into the work you do with your students?

11. Miranda Chavez demonstrates the power of engaging her students in a social-action project that reflects the needs of the local community in which she works rather than focusing on more global

issues such as saving the rainforest. Why might this community-based work be more powerful for her students?

12. Ramón Martinez states, "Critical educators must . . . step up and take a stand. In defense of educational justice and sound pedagogy, we must engage in individual and collective resistance. If we truly seek to empower our students, we must begin to challenge the educational policies that harm them" (pp. 444–445). Some argue that in order to be a social-justice teacher, you must also engage in your own activism. Do you believe this to be true? Why or why not?

13. Do the statements of Dewey, West, Havel, and others cited in this chapter add to your concerns or worries about becoming a teacher; do they make becoming a teacher seem less worrisome; do the statements engender both concern and hope? Explain.

Too Angry and Too Hopeful to Leave

14. Explain why you would like to be a teacher.

WEB SITES

You can link directly to all of the Web sites listed below from the *Teaching to Change the World* Web site located at www.mhhe.com/oakes2e. We recommend linking from that site, as URLs are subject to change and we will be posting updates there.

- http://www.teachingforchange.org/http://www.te achingforchange.org/——**Teaching for Change** is a Washington, DC-based not-for-profit organization that promotes social and economic justice through public education. The site offers an online catalog for hundreds of books, videos, and posters for the K-12 classroom. In addition, this site provides sources for a critical analysis of current issues in the news and links connect you to many more progressive organizations and publishers.

- http://www.teachingtochangela.org——**Teaching to Change** LA is an online journal of IDEA, **UCLA's Institute for Democracy, Education, and Access.** Here you will find the work and thought of educators, students, parents, and activists who confront the most critical issues that schools and communities face across greater Los Angeles.

- http://www.rethinkingschools.org/index.html— An online **Urban Educational Journal** firmly committed to **equity and to the vision that public education is central to the creation of a humane, caring, multiracial democracy.** While writing for a broad audience, Rethinking Schools emphasizes problems facing urban schools, particularly issues of race. It is an activist publication, with articles written by and for teachers, parents, and students.

- http://www.glsen.org/templates/index.html— **GLSEN—Gay, Lesbian and Straight Education Network.** Founded as a volunteer group in Boston in 1990, GLSEN has grown into one of the nation's leading voices for equality and safety in the educational system.

- http://www.nameorg.org——**National Association for Multicultural Education.** Founded in 1990, NAME provides resources and support that help educators promote "a philosophy of inclusion that embraces the basic tenets of cultural pluralism," and "promoting cultural and ethnic diversity as a national strength."

http://members.aol.com/nceaweb—NCEA—National Coalition of Education Activists. A network of teacher, parent, and community activists who organize around social-justice issues in schools and communities.